The web wizard's guide to DISCARD Freeware and shareware

The Web Wizard's Guide to Freeware and Shareware

Wendy Lehnert

OAKTON COMMUNITY COLLEGE
DES PLAINES CAMPUS
1600 EAST GOLF ROAD
DES PLAINES, IL 60016

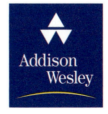

Addison
Wesley

Boston San Francisco New York
London Toronto Sydney Tokyo Singapore Madrid
Mexico City Munich Paris Cape Town Hong Kong Montreal

Executive Editor: *Susan Hartman Sullivan*
Associate Managing Editor: *Pat Mahtani*
Executive Marketing Manager: *Michael Hirsch*
Production Supervision: *Diane Freed*
Cover and Interior Designer: *Leslie Haimes*
Composition: *Gillian Hall, The Aardvark Group*
Copyeditor: *Betsy Hardinger*
Cover Design: *Gina Hagen Kolenda*
Proofreader: *Holly McLean-Aldis*
Prepress and Manufacturing: *Caroline Fell*

Access the latest information about Addison-Wesley titles from our World Wide Web site: *http://www.aw.com/cs*

Many of the designations used by manufacturers and sellers to distinguish their products are claimed as trademarks. Where those designations appear in this book, and Addison-Wesley was aware of a trademark claim, the designations have been printed in initial caps or all caps.

The programs and applications presented in this book have been included for their instructional value. They have been tested with care, but are not guaranteed for any particular purpose. The publisher does not offer any warranties or representations, not does it accept any liabilities with respect to the programs or applications.

Library of Congress Cataloging-in-Publication Data
Lehnert, Wendy G.
The Web Wizard's guide to Freeware and Shareware / Wendy Lehnert.
p. cm.
Includes bibliographical references and index.
ISBN 0-201-74171-7 (pbk.)
1. Free computer software--Computer network resources I. Title.

QA76.754.L45 2002
005.3--dc21

2001045826
CIP

12345678910—QWT—04030201

TABLE OF CONTENTS

PREFACE

About Addison-Wesley's Web Wizard Series

The beauty of the Web is that, with a little effort, anyone can harness its power to create sophisticated Web sites. Addison-Wesley's Web Wizard Series helps students master the Web by presenting a concise introduction to one important Internet topic or technology in each book. The books start from square one and assume no prior experience with the technology being covered. Mastering the Web doesn't come with a wave of a magic wand; but by studying these accessible, highly visual textbooks, readers will be well on their way.

The series is written by instructors who are familiar with the challenges beginners face when learning the material. To this end, the Web Wizard books offer more than a cookbook approach: they emphasize principles and offer clear explanations, giving the reader a strong foundation of knowledge on which to build.

Numerous features highlight important points and aid in learning:

⭐ Tips — important points to keep in mind

⭐ Shortcuts — timesaving ideas

⭐ Warnings — things to watch out for

⭐ Do It Yourself — activities to try now

⭐ Review questions and hands-on exercises

⭐ Online references — Web sites to visit to obtain more information

Supplementary materials for the books, including updates, additional examples, and source code, are available at `http://www.aw.com/webwizard`. Also available for qualified instructors adopting a book from the series are instructor's manuals, sample tests, and solutions. Please contact your Addison-Wesley sales representative for the instructor resources password.

About This Book

Newcomers to the Internet are well-advised to lurk and learn about the culture of the Internet before diving in head first. In most cases, this amounts to learning basic Netiquette and remembering that the Internet cuts across geographical and cultural boundaries. But in some cases, a cultural presence on the Internet does not correspond to a geographical, ethnic, or religious population. In particular, the culture of computer programmers has created a world of high-quality software that is freely distributed over the Internet.

Most people who routinely use the Internet for e-mail and Web browsing have no idea just how much valuable software is available online at little or no cost. Moreover, you don't have to be a programmer to take advantage of these software resources. With the guidance in this book, anyone can learn how to download and install software from the Internet without fear. One is well-advised to be on guard for computer viruses and other potential dangers, and we will show you what you need to do to stay safe. We'll also walk you through the usual downloading and installation routines, so you'll always know what to expect in any software scenario you'll encounter.

If you are primarily interesting in Web design, you'll be pleased to discover a world of HTML editors, graphics programs, FTP clients, special-purpose tools, and time-saving utilities. Most of this software is distributed for free or a nominal licensing fee, and cannot be purchased in stores. Students on a budget will be especially pleased to see that they do not have to forego regular meals in order to pursue Web design skills using state-of-the-art software.

Programmers have always used the Internet to share their software, and this culture of freely shared resources predates the commercialization of personal computer software. We'll explain what's legal, what's not, and how to find the best that the Net has to offer.

Anyone can take advantage of freeware and shareware on the Internet—it's easy, and it's fun to experiment with new software. With the right software, your computer will make your work go faster and your recreational activities truly recreational. In fact, your computer may even feel exciting again. If you haven't been exploring software on the Internet, you're missing out on one of the Net's greatest secrets.

This book was inspired by hundreds of undergraduates at the University of Massachusetts at Amherst who have come to me looking to learn as much as they can about the Internet. Although Web page construction was always near the top of the to-do list for most of these students, not many of them knew about the software resources that are available online. As a result, the topic of freeware and shareware has always been a pleasant surprise for the students in my Internet courses. This book was written for students everywhere who simply want to find out how they can benefit from the resources of the Internet.

I am thankful to my acquisitions editor, Susan Hartman Sullivan for suggesting that I write this book for the Web Wizard series. I am also very grateful for the able and knowledgeable efforts of my copy editor, Betsy Hardinger, who enhanced the quality of this manuscript. Also, many thanks to Diane Freed for her expert production management and to Gillian Hall, whose first-rate typesetting skills have made these pages so visually appealing.

My reviewers were also very helpful in suggesting directions and priorities, which are all the more important for a short book in order to keep it short:

Jane Ostrander, DeAnza College
Michael Gildersleeve, University of New Hampshire
Stephanie Ludi, Arizona State University
David Fisher, University of Massachusetts
Martin Granier, Western Washington University

I am also especially indebted to David Fisher whose careful concern for accuracy at all levels has saved me from countless missteps, both online and off. As always, any errors or omissions in these pages are my responsibility alone. Credit for the rest is gratefully shared with everyone else.

Wendy Lehnert
October 2001

SOFTWARE ON THE INTERNET

Newcomers to the Internet are often surprised to discover that a wealth of software is available online. Then when they find out how much of that software is free—*and perfectly legal*—they are mystified. Some are incredulous. If it's free, it seems that there must be something wrong with it—there's got to be a catch. In this chapter you'll explore the world of software and find out what everyone needs to know about software on the Internet.

CHAPTER ONE

Chapter Objectives

⭐ To understand how the Internet has influenced programmers and the process of software design

⭐ To understand the difference between shareware and freeware

⭐ To learn how software licenses protect software authors as well as software users

◎◎ Software, Programmers, and the Internet

The world of software can be broken into various categories. The most familiar category is **commercial** software, also known as **shrink-wrap** software because of the tight-fitting plastic packages it comes in. Commercial software is a commodity just like cars or clothing. It is sold for profit, often by salespeople, and usually in stores. Commercial software that was new and exciting a year ago is often dated and sold at a discount today (just like cars and clothing).

Programmers have their own categories, including **firmware** (programs permanently written onto a hardware device), **middleware** (software that passes data from one application to another application), and **vaporware** (a tongue-in-cheek term for commercial software that has been announced but does not yet exist).

Consumers usually don't need to describe their software using programmer jargon, but everyone who owns a personal computer should know about freeware and shareware. **Freeware** is software distributed to users at no charge, usually over the Internet but sometimes on a CD in a book or a magazine. **Shareware** is not free, but it's usually inexpensive ($10–$30) and can be used for free during a trial period, typically three to eight weeks. Shareware is usually distributed over the Internet.

Commercial software, freeware, and shareware aren't really software categories as much as they are **software distribution models**.

This book is all about freeware and shareware—how to find it, what to do with it, and everything else you need to know about it—so we'll circle back to a longer description of freeware and shareware shortly. But before we dive into the how-to's of freeware and shareware, let's first look into some of the why's behind these alternatives to commercial software. Why would anyone give something away if they could make money selling it? To understand this, you need to understand a little about the psychology of computer programmers and how the Internet reinforces a programming culture in which software always was, and always will be, something more than a commodity.

☆**TIP**   **Computer Programmers, Software Engineers, and Code**

This book uses the term **computer programmer**, a casual version of **software engineer**, the preferred term for formal job descriptions. *Computer programmer* shortens conveniently to a single word (*programmer*), which is much more accurate than the analogous shorthand for software engineer (*engineer*). So I talk about computer programmers, or just plain programmers, instead of software engineers. Similarly, I sometimes refer to computer programs as **code**, which is shorthand for the **executable code** or **executable files** that programmers write.

A Tradition of Openness

The Internet wasn't covered by the popular press much before 1990. However, its origins date back to 1970, when four computers—at the Stanford Research Institute, the University of California at Los Angeles, the University of California at Santa Barbara, and the University of Utah at Salt Lake City—were first hooked up over phone lines. This tiny network marked the beginning of the **ARPAnet**, the earliest ancestor of today's Internet. The network got its name from the **Advanced Research Projects Agency** (ARPA) of the Department of Defense. Twenty years of concerted effort by computer scientists and engineers has since created an all-purpose global network for high-speed digital communications. This same period also witnessed the creation and commercialization of PCs, which made it possible for anyone to hop on the Internet from the convenience of their own home. No one in 1970 could have imagined the Internet of today. There was never a master plan in place to guide all the contributing technologies.

Although there was no grand plan in mind, a sense of limitless possibilities attracted a generation of scientists and technicians to the field of computer science, where innovation is a way of life and nothing stands still for long. Until the early 1990s, the Internet was used primarily by scientists and academics pursuing long-distance collaborations and scholarly research. Computer science students and professional programmers also used the Internet for casual communications and have been responsible for much of the software that makes the Internet what it is today.

> ☆**TIP**   **The Invention of E-Mail**
>
> Ray Tomlinson sent the first e-mail message across the ARPAnet in 1971. No one documented the event because it didn't seem very important at the time. It wasn't sponsored by a research grant or dignified by a formal software development project. Instead, it was the work of one lone programmer who thought that informal person-to-person communications via networked computers might be a handy little hack. (In those days, **hackers** were good guys and a **hack** was a clever bit of original code casually tossed together in a day or two.)

ARPA sponsored much of the software development associated with the Internet's early years, and it was quick to leverage these efforts so that each ARPA-sponsored research lab could benefit from the resources of all the others. If a university researcher needed to run some software that was available only on a computer at a different university, that researcher could use the Internet to run the required software remotely, via an Internet application called **telnet**. And if a programmer at one ARPA-sponsored lab wrote a useful software utility that would be handy for programmers at the other labs, the files for that software could be made available to all authorized personnel via an Internet application called the **File Transfer Protocol** (FTP). Telnet was created in 1969, and FTP was first used in 1971. Both applications, still in use, were instrumental in the evolution of an Internet culture predicated on shared resources.

ARPA-sponsored research has always been conducted at university research laboratories and a handful of private companies dedicated to basic research. The ARPAnet was created to explore the operation of computer networks and to facilitate shared resources among ARPA-sponsored research groups. Although this research was sponsored by the Department of Defense, it was carried out mostly in American universities, where scientists communicate their ideas freely and openly with anyone. Computer scientists who wanted to use a computer network but who were not funded by ARPA soon created their own computer network, CSnet. In 1982, a gateway was established to connect the ARPAnet with CSnet, and the term **Internet** was adopted as a shorthand for "internetworked communication." The grandest network of networks was born, and computer scientists used it freely to exchange ideas, data, results, and feedback.

No one cared whether Internet communications were secure. The university tradition of open communication prevailed, and innovative research thrived in this first online community of top-rate scientists. Computers used by the Pentagon for military purposes were never part of the ARPAnet or its Internet offspring. The research community and the military community had very different needs, and there was never any move to consolidate their computational resources. Classified documents never found their way onto the Internet, and the vast majority of the research associated with computer networking was never classified (most universities prohibit doctoral dissertations based on classified research).

Thus, the researchers and programmers who dominated the early Internet established a tradition of openly shared ideas and resources, and software was at the center of this tradition. Computer science students and programmers working on research grants were rewarded for work that influenced others, and software was freely posted for public consumption to encourage widespread experimentation and validation. Programmers did not take jobs at universities in order to get rich; instead, university jobs were attractive because they put people at the cutting edge of research. Software developed in academic settings was an intellectual undertaking, whereas software developed for the commercial sector was something else entirely. The best and the brightest wanted to tackle the challenges of transforming computer technologies, and the spirit of basic research dominated the whole enterprise.

The Rise of Commercial Software

It would be a while before the dot-com explosion transformed computer programming into an option for the get-rich-quick crowd, but by then the intellectual foundations for excellence in computer programming were firmly entrenched. No one rises very far in the world of programming without a lot of hard work and study, and the shift from academic programming to commercial programming is anything but subtle. Computer science departments (where one learns academic programming) teach the scientific principles behind the programming enterprise, whereas certification courses (where one learns commercial programming) teach only what industry needs today. Academic know-how endures, but commercial skills meet job requirements.

Because most commercial programmers hold undergraduate degrees in computer science, most of them straddle two worlds: They learned their craft in academia, but they practice it in a very different one. Academic programming assignments are used as a learning tool to drive home new concepts, and students are encouraged to play around and experiment. In contrast, professional programming assignments must meet rigorous specifications for the sake of producing a usable commercial product. Playful experimentation is a waste of time. The shift from a computer science classroom to a corporate environment is not always easy.

Commercial programmers experience the disconnect in their programming lives long after their university years. To them, it makes sense to separate recreational programming activities from professional programming duties. Nondisclosure agreements might rule during working hours, but programs written on personal

☆ **TIP**   In Chapter Six we'll return to the concept of free software and see how some programmers have found a way to make a living writing it.

time using personal equipment are beyond the reach of corporate lawyers. And when software developed on personal time is deemed worthy, it can be distributed on the Internet for the good of the larger community—just as software has been freely distributed since the earliest days of the ARPAnet. As long as there are free programmers, there will always be free software.

Getting Software over the Internet

The Internet has also changed the way commercial software manufacturers do business. It's more expensive to produce and distribute shrink-wrap software through retail outlets than to distribute it over the Internet. As a result, the same software is often available through both channels, but the shrink-wrap version is more expensive. For the extra money you get your software on a CD-ROM along with printed documentation that you hope you won't have to read. But the CD-ROM software may not be the latest version available, and you won't know that unless you've checked the manufacturer's Web site for the latest updates. Almost every manufacturer that distributes software on CD-ROMs has a Web site where the same software is distributed via the Internet.

On many sites you can download the complete software package, or a limited edition version, for a free 30-day trial. You can do the same thing with competing software offerings for the sake of serious comparison shopping. Once you've tried the samples, you can decide which one is right for you and purchase a software license online.

☆ **SHORTCUT**   **Special Edition Distributions**

Software manufacturers often give away **special edition** (also called **limited edition** or **demo**) software so that you can try it out and see if you like it. Typically, these distributions don't have all the features of the complete edition, but they are good for review purposes. You may be content to stay with the special edition, or you may feel it's worthwhile to purchase the full version. Either way, you can find out whether you like the software before you buy it.

Software distribution sites encourage ongoing communication between manufacturers and customers, and they streamline customer support. If there are any bugs in the software, you may be able to find manufacturer's software **patches** that you can install to fix the bugs. New software releases or updates may become available to registered users over the Web, often before the shrink-wrap versions make it into the stores.

If you feel bad about not having a hardcopy user manual, you probably shouldn't. Online documentation and help files are usually at least as good as the hardcopy versions. A searchable help facility is almost always easier to work with than the index in a large user manual. In addition, it's always easier to get up-to-date corrections and additions on a Web site. If you have any problems with your software, the manufacturer may sponsor an online technical support discussion group where users can discuss their problems with one another as well as the company's tech support staff. Tech support via e-mail is another welcome feature for those who do not like to be put on hold when they call an 800 number for help.

Shareware and Freeware

Thousands of Web sites post software that you can download to your computer with a few keystrokes or a single mouse click (see Figure 1.1). A commercial site may or may not ask you to register before you download. Each site is set up a little differently. In Chapter Two you'll learn how to find software online and how to protect your computer from computer viruses when you add new software. For now, let's look at the two most popular software distribution models: shareware and freeware.

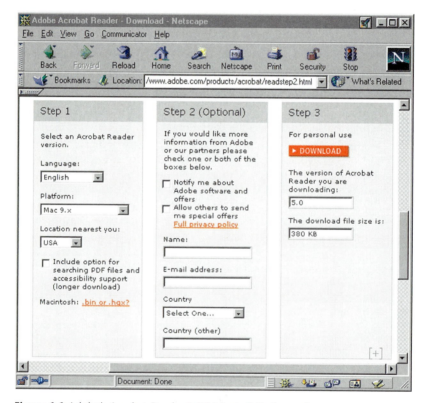

Figure 1.1 Adobe's Acrobat Reader Is Distributed Online as Freeware

Shareware is distributed at no cost over the Internet for evaluation. The trial period is usually 21 to 30 days, sometimes as much as 60 days. You're free to use the software as much as you want, and then when the trial period is over, you're asked to make a decision. If you don't like the software, you delete it from your computer and that's the end of it. But if you like it enough to keep using it, you're asked to pay for it. Payments are usually made by credit card via a secure Web page or 800 number.

Often, payments depend on the honor system. If you want to cheat, that's between you and your conscience. In other cases, the software keeps track of how many days have gone by, and something special happens when the trial period is up. The software may make one last plea for payment, and if no payment is made, the software **self-destructs** (refuses to execute). In other cases, it refuses to launch until you type a special alphanumeric string called a **registration key**. Registration keys are usually sent to paying customers via e-mail. Figure 1.2 shows how people who have purchased a copy of GetRight can enter their registration key by clicking an Enter Code button.

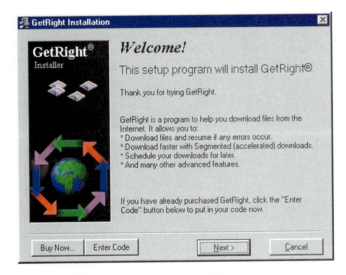

Figure 1.2 A Registration Key Is Proof of Payment

When you purchase a software license for software obtained from the Internet, you may be given a special **uniform resource locator** (URL), a Web address where you can download the registered version of the software. Or you may receive a registration key that unlocks the registered version (which is already on your computer, hiding inside the trial version).

Some shareware shows you a reminder each time you launch the software during the examination period (see Figure 1.3). Shareware that reminds you to register each time you use it is called **nagware**. The reminders are called **nag screens**.

Manufacturers of nagware hope that you will do the right thing if you're reminded often enough (at every possible opportunity). Some nagware actually allows you to keep using the software after the trial has expired. They keep reminding you that you have passed the deadline and you really should pay for the software. You can ignore these reminders, but sooner or later guilt sets in or you get so tired of seeing the nag screen that you give in and do the right thing.

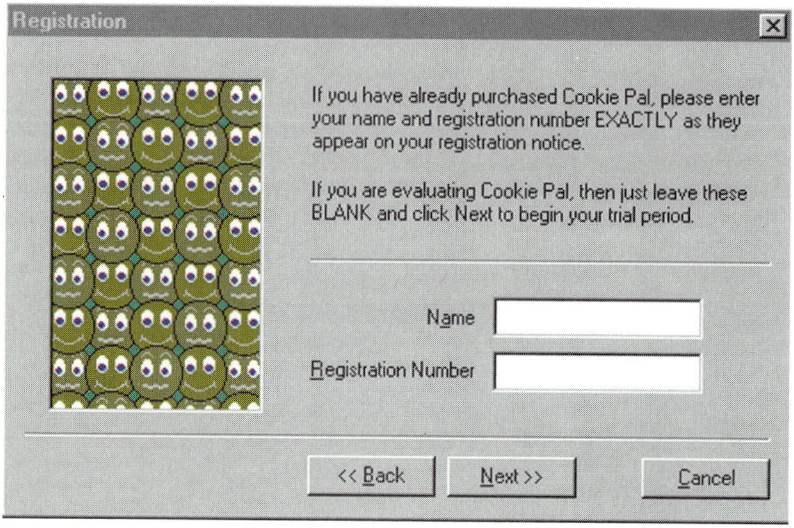

Figure 1.3 Nagware Reminders Pop Up Each Time You Launch the Software

Shareware that self-destructs when your time is up is perhaps more effective at making people pony up, although some people might feel vaguely offended by the heavy-handedness of this approach. It's not unreasonable from the merchants' point of view—they're simply protecting their inventory from shoplifters. After all, how many retailers are willing to let you take an item home for 30 days at no charge so that you can make sure you really like it?

Adware is a variation on nagware. Instead of badgering you with nag screens, adware badgers you with advertisements. If you want the ads to stop, you can pay for the software and get a version that runs without ads. But if you don't mind the ads, you can run the software as adware as long as you want.

Some manufacturers withhold useful features from their trial version in the hope that you will like what you see well enough to pay for the registered version. The trial version is still usable. Typically, it's missing at least one key feature that is either a big time-saver or just highly desirable.

Newcomers to the Internet are often surprised to discover how much freeware is given away over the Net. It's natural to assume that such software must not be very good, but that's not necessarily true. Some freeware is every bit as good as its more costly commercial counterparts. Freeware may be distributed at no charge for many different reasons. A company may simply want to increase traffic on its Web site, so it uses a modest piece of freeware as a come-on. Sometimes the software is not so modest. Microsoft and Netscape, for example, have been giving away their browsers for years in a bid to establish market dominance. Many companies distribute their software as freeware to students or anyone using the software for personal use, while deriving a revenue stream from users in the workplace. This shareware/freeware approach to commercial/noncommercial users makes it possible to maximize a user base while maintaining a stable income stream based on corporate users.

A company must have deep pockets to give away an important product for years just to establish a market position. But at the other end of the spectrum, a freelance programmer who is reworking a piece of software may want to get feedback from many users during its development (**beta**) phase. Or a novice programmer may find it gratifying to see other people using his personal creation even if no money is involved.

Still other programmers distribute freeware as an act of guerilla warfare against old-order economic forces. The authors of the Napster and Wrapster programs, which facilitate MP3 file sharing, were opposed to the commercial interests of the Recording Industry Association of America (RIAA), so they freely distributed their software to undermine RIAA. In such situations, the expression *computer revolution* is more than a metaphor for social upheaval. Industries can rise and fall as new technologies become available over the Internet.

◎◎ Understanding Software Licenses

When you acquire a piece of software you become a software **user**, with the rights and responsibilities set forth in the licensing agreement. You do not own the software even if you have paid for it; you have acquired only a right to use the software, subject to the restrictions of the software license.

Whenever you obtain new software, it is your legal responsibility to know what the licensing agreement says. This is not a joyous responsibility for most people. If you routinely ignore software licenses, you are not alone. The language is stiff, the restrictions are predictable, and the disclaimers are unsettling. How many products are accompanied by contractual agreements in which the manufacturer disavows all responsibility for any catastrophic consequences associated with the use of the product?

Still, these much maligned and often ignored documents are the only barriers that stand between software manufacturers and financial ruin. **Software piracy**—the unauthorized copying and distribution of software—is the bane of commercial software, and software licenses are notoriously difficult for companies to enforce. If you install a piece of software on two computers when the license restricts you to one, the police are not likely to show up at your door with a search warrant. But if you use a CD burner to create a few hundred bootlegged copies of the same software, that's a dif-

> ☆**WARNING** **A Software License Is a Binding Contract**
>
> You don't have to sign a piece of paper to enter into a legally binding contract. With software licenses, it may be enough to open an envelope or break a seal. If you're using software that was distributed with a licensing agreement, you are legally bound by its terms whether or not you've read it. Read your software licenses. They're not all the same, and you're responsible for knowing what they say.

ferent story. Most of us think we understand which lines can and can't be crossed, so we ignore software licenses, use good common sense, and steer clear of anything that looks risky.

Software licenses can test the ethics of even the straightest arrows among us. Consider the following scenarios.

The Desktop/Laptop Dilemma

Suppose the license for your favorite word processing program says you're allowed to install it on only one computer at one time. But you have a desktop computer that you use most of the time and a laptop that you use when you travel, and you want to use the same software on both machines without having to uninstall and install it each time you take a trip. The licensing restriction seems nuts. You don't intend to use both installations simultaneously, and that must be what the license is trying to prohibit. Do you have the right to take liberties with the license restrictions as long as you adhere to their intent?

The Seven-Year-Old Software Pirate

Suppose your seven-year-old daughter has spent the day at a friend's house playing a computer game. She comes home with the CD-ROM for the game and asks you to install it so that she can play it at home. You know this can't be legal, but your daughter wants it *now*, and she's not going to be happy if you tell her she must wait until you can purchase your own copy. The issue is complicated by the fact that her friends routinely share their computer games and you're the only parent who is uneasy about the practice. Do you have the right to install the "bootlegged" software now, as long as you intend to purchase your own copy? What if your daughter loses interest in the game and forgets all about it after two days? Do you handle this differently if the software costs $5 or $50? Should the price enter into your reasoning?

The Garage Sale Software Deal

You've been browsing at a garage sale (or a flea market or eBay), where someone is offering a popular piece of commercial software for a bargain price. She explains that it's used software, but it comes with all the original documentation and packaging. Is it legal for her to resell commercial software like this? What if she has burned a backup CD and is still using the software? How can you know whether she's breaking the licensing agreement by selling the software? Can you be fined or arrested for entering into an illegal transaction if you don't know that it's illegal?

Millions of computer owners face these ethical and legal conundrums every day. Some software manufacturers have acknowledged the difficulty of their licensing restrictions and have taken steps to set things right. For example, some licensing agreements clarify the desktop/laptop dilemma and loosen the restrictions to accommodate consumers who travel.

But other dilemmas remain. One way to solve the problem is to remove all unreasonable or unenforceable restrictions and give end users the right to use and redistribute software freely. Although this strategy may sound radical and incapable of supporting the people who write software for a living, it is an alternative model for commercial software and one that is actually being used by advocates of **open source** software (see Chapter Six).

> ⭐**WARNING** Buying and Selling Used Software
>
> Used software can be legally resold as long as the seller does not retain a copy and does include all the original documentation. Stores that buy and sell used software are generally adept at spotting pirated software, so anything you buy in a store is probably being transferred legally. A large secondary market exists for computer games, and a somewhat less robust market for business software. If you find software at a flea market, look for a CD with the manufacturer's label and complete documentation. Hand-written labels on CDs are a sure sign of pirated software, as are CDs without documentation.

If you are new to the world of freeware and shareware, you'll be pleased to know that not all licensing agreements are written by lawyers. Some are written by plain-speaking people with no training in legalese. These agreements are often written with humor, humility, and originality. If you happen to hit on one of the better ones, it might be the high point of your day.

The typical freeware license includes standard legal disclaimers and a few restrictions on secondary distribution. For example, it may be all right to pass the program to friends but only if the executable is bundled with a README document or if specific comments are left intact in a source code file. Other freeware licenses flatly prohibit users from redistributing the software under any circumstances.

Some freeware licenses add a quirky twist. Many programmers want to hear from their users, so they ask only for a quick e-mail note in return for their software. Such freeware is called **emailware**. When an author requests a postcard in exchange for software, it's called **postcardware**. If you look at enough freeware licenses you may see variations on these ideas. For example, Jilles Groenendijk, the author of PhonConv, requests an item or postcard related to Garfield (a cartoon character) in return for his software.

To see a unique licensing agreement, check out the **careware** license for Arachnophilia. The author, Paul Lutus, explains that his licensing agreement is wholly negotiable, and he will take anything except money. Would-be users are free to suggest their own terms, but Lutus is hoping for "the really remarkable transactions, which you recognize instinctively when you see them." To make things a little clearer, he gives an example of careware payment contract:

> *For example, here is a payment I will accept for a copy of Arachnophilia.*
>
> *To own Arachnophilia, I ask that you stop whining about how hard your life is, at least for a while. When Americans whine, nearly everybody else in the world laughs. ...*
>
> *Every time we whine about how tough we have it, apart from the fact that we look ridiculous, we make it harder for people around us to appreciate how much we have. We encourage people to overlook the things we do have, the gifts of man and nature. We provide a context to dismiss everything as not good enough, to be miserable in the midst of plenty. ...*
>
> *So here is my deal: stop whining for an hour, a day, a week, your choice, and you will have earned your copy of Arachnophilia. Say encouraging words to young people, make them feel welcome on the planet Earth (many do not). Show by example that we don't need all we have in order to be happy and productive.*

If this is not the most thought-provoking software licensing agreement in existence, it must surely be in the top 10.

In short, whenever you download freeware and shareware from the Net, be sure to read the licensing agreements. Some may surprise you, and some may make you smile, but they are all legally binding documents. It is your responsibility to know what they say.

★ TIP   Site Licenses

If you're a university student or commercial employee, you may be able to obtain commercial software at a reduced rate through a **site license**. Organizations can often purchase a site license that gives them the right to distribute 10, 50, or 100 (or more) copies to authorized people (usually students or employees). Sometimes, site-licensed software is distributed free or for a nominal fee. If you are affiliated with an institution where large numbers of people work with computers, check to see if any software is available to you through a site license.

⭐ Summary

▶ University-based research laboratories established a tradition for software development based on open communication and shared resources, a tradition that was reinforced by the Internet.

▶ Shareware can be used for free during a trial period but is subject to licensing fees after the trial period is over. Freeware is distributed at no cost but may still be subject to legal restrictions.

▶ Software licenses apply to freeware and shareware on the Internet as well as shrink-wrap software distributed through retail outlets. Software users are legally responsible for understanding the terms and restrictions of their software licenses.

⭐ Online References

Internet History.
http://www.isoc.org/internet/history/

Freeware: The Heart and Soul of the Internet.
http://www.oreilly.com/news/freeware_0398.html

The History of Shareware and PsL.
http://www.pslweb.com/history.htm

Information Wants to Be Free.
http://www.anu.edu.au/people/Roger.Clarke/II/IWtbF.html

Understanding Software Licenses.
http://allbusiness.com/cmt/information/general.jsp?fname=201

⭐ Review Questions

1. Who sponsored the early research behind the Internet? Where was most of this research conducted?

2. What is special edition software?

3. What is shareware?

4. What is nagware?

5. Explain why a programmer might distribute a computer program as freeware.

6. Explain why a software company might distribute a program as freeware.

7. Explain what a registration key is and how it is used.

8. When you purchase software, what exactly are you buying? Do you own the software?

9. If you obtain freeware from the Internet, can you legally pass it on to your friends? Explain your answer.

10. Under what conditions is it legal to resell used software?

★ Hands-On Exercises

1. Visit `http://www.pretext.com/mar98/features/story2.htm` and find out what the first e-mail message said. Where did this message originate? Where was it sent to?

2. Adobe's Acrobat Reader is a freeware version of Adobe Acrobat. Visit `http://www.adobe.com/` and find out how much Adobe Acrobat costs. What is the main difference between Adobe Acrobat Reader and Adobe Acrobat?

3. Go to `http://home.netscape.com/home/license.html` and read the old licensing agreement once used by Netscape Communications Corporation. Under what circumstances was the software for this license distributed as freeware? (Note: At the time of this writing, Netscape's stand-alone browser is being distributed as freeware without restriction.)

4. Visit `http://www.poznaklaw.com/articles/netact.htm` and read about the NET Act. What are the penalties for software piracy under the NET Act? What legal loophole did this legislation close? What is the statute of limitations for a software piracy prosecution?

5. Visit `http://www.microsoft.com/piracy/atrisk/faq/default.asp` to find out what Microsoft has to say about the laptop dilemma. Under what conditions can Microsoft software be installed on a portable laptop computer in addition to a desktop computer? Note: This page may not display correctly under Netscape Navigator because of HTML errors.

CHAPTER TWO

DOWNLOADING AND INSTALLING SOFTWARE

When you know where to go and what precautions to take, you can explore the exciting world of commercial software, shareware, and freeware on your home computer. If you own your own computer and you haven't been sampling software on the Internet, you're missing out on a big part of what the Internet has to offer. In this chapter you'll learn everything there is to know about software downloads and safe installation practices. If you're new to this, you'll be surprised to see how easy it is. If you're more experienced, you might want to skim this chapter for tips and tricks that can make downloading smoother and faster.

Chapter Objectives

⭐ To find out where to look for good software on the Internet

⭐ To become familiar with downloading procedures

⭐ To learn how to deal with various software installation scenarios

☆ To discover how to work with file utilities and file archives

☆ To learn what precautions you need to take to steer clear of computer viruses

---

☆WARNING Before You Start

Before you add any new software to your computer, make sure you read this entire chapter. In particular, make sure you understand how to scan a software download for computer viruses, how to protect your privacy online, and how to uninstall new software if you decide you don't want to keep it.

◎◎ Where to Look for Software

The Web has made it easy to find and obtain software. You just need to know where to look. Whenever you download an executable file from the Internet, you should go to the Web site of either a reputable commercial software manufacturer or a large, well-known software clearinghouse. A **software clearinghouse** is a Web site that specializes in online software distributions.

Many software clearinghouses index large collections of downloadable software in searchable **subject trees** (a list of topics that branch off into subtopics). Most of them also let you search by keywords. Some include a brief description of each software item, and a few include software ratings, download counts, and e-mail newsletters to keep you on top of the best new software. Some software clearinghouses are components of larger Web **portals** (large Web sites offering a variety of resources), and others are dedicated sites that concentrate only on software (see Figure 2.1).

☆WARNING Know Your Software Sources

Never download executable files from personal Web pages, mail messages (even if they appear to come from a trusted source), Usenet newsgroup articles, message boards, chat rooms, IRC channels, or instant message sessions. Computer viruses and other forms of malicious software are often planted in offbeat places to trap the unwary. You can recognize executable files by looking at the **file extension** (the last part) of the file name. An executable file for Windows usually ends in .exe and an executable file for the Macintosh usually ends in .bin.

Just as it pays to try out several search engines before you decide on your favorites, it makes sense to visit a number of software clearinghouses to find the ones that are best for you. Each clearinghouse has its own features and mix of software titles. Some clearinghouses specialize in programs for a particular population (such as Web designers), and others focus on a specific software type (such as Java applets). Some are easier to navigate than others, and some have larger software collections than others.

If you have time on your hands, it's fun to visit clearinghouses to see what they have to offer. Even if two clearinghouses cover much of the same software, you may like the reviews at one site better, or you may enjoy a special feature at one site.

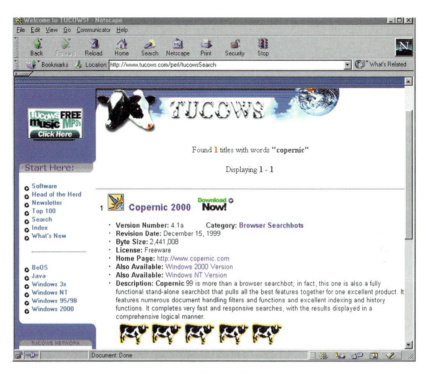

Figure 2.1 Tucows.com is a Popular Software Clearinghouse

Popular Software Sites

Following is a list of clearinghouses that you may find useful.

Tucows (http://www.tucows.com)

Tucows offers a massive collection of software with many special features, including the famous five-cow rating system. Check out the editorials (follow the News link from the home page) and the tutorials under HTML Stuff. Tucows has a lot of **mirror** sites (identical copies of the Tucows site stored at different Web locations). If you're asked to pick a region, try one close to home; some mirror sites are faster than others. At times, Tucows may seem difficult to navigate, although it does get easier with a little practice. Tucows includes Macintosh software, but there are better software clearinghouses for Macs.

DOWNLOAD.COM (http://download.cnet.com)

This is CNet's download site (CNet is a Web portal for tech types). You navigate this site using keyword searches. Pull-down menus let you filter your search results for a specific operating system, general software category, and license type (such as freeware). Take a look at CNet's list of software-related newsletters. This is an excellent site for both PC and Mac users.

ZDNet Downloads (http://www.zdnet.com/downloads/)

ZDNet is a Web portal for software junkies. Once you get hooked on software downloads, you may want to make this page your default home page. You can filter your searches for PCs, Macs, Palm Pilots, or CE laptops. If you set the filter for "all ZDNet," your keyword search will return **hits** (matches) not only for software downloads but also for product reviews, tips and help articles, tech news, commentary, and more. Each of these hit lists is displayed separately, so you can scan them or ignore them as you wish. The different hit lists make this is a great browsing site.

Dave Central Software Archive (http://www.davecentral.com)

A large site with personality and some useful features. Check out the free animated GIF of the day and the free font of the day. This is a site for PC and Linux users, but even Mac users can grab the GIF of the day.

> ★**SHORTCUT**   If you enjoy browsing software clearinghouses, bookmark your favorite software sites. The ones listed here are only the beginning.

MACDOWNLOAD.COM
(http://www.zdnet.com/mac/download.html)

This is the Macintosh side of the ZDNet portal. It's a great place to go for Mac software.

SHAREWARE.COM (http://shareware.cnet.com/)

This is CNet's meta search engine for shareware. Use the pull-down menu to filter your search results for a specific platform.

Other Software Sites

Here's a list of other good sites where you can download Windows software.

★ http://www.webattack.com/

★ http://www.getyoursfree.com/

★ http://www.mysharewarepage.com/webtools.htm

★ http://www.completelyfreesoftware.com/

★ http://www.nonags.com/

★ http://www.Slaughterhouse.com/pick.html

★ http://www.completelyfreesoftware.com/index_all.html

★ http://www.32bit.com/

★ http://www.freewareweb.com/

★ http://www.thefreesite.com/

★ http://www.rocketdownload.com

★ http://www.hotfiles.com/

★ http://www.winmag.com

★ http://softsite.com/

★ http://happypuppy.com/

★ http://newapps.internet.com/categories.html

☆ `http://www.galttech.com/sharware.shtml`

☆ `http://cws.internet.com/`

☆ `http://www.netigen.com/freeware.html`

If you're a Macintosh user, check out these sites:

☆ `http://www.macresource.com/mrp/software.shtml`

☆ `http://www.macorchard.com/`

☆ `http://www.chezmark.com/`

☆ `http://www.macupdate.com/`

☆ `http://hyperarchive.lcs.mit.edu/HyperArchive/`

☆ `http://asu.info.apple.com/`

☆ `http://www.versiontracker.com/`

☆ `http://www.tidbits.com/iskm/iskm-soft.html`

☆ `http://Macs.Bon.Net/MacFreeware_Os_1024x768.html`

If you're nervous about downloading software from the Internet and you think it's safer to buy software from your friendly local retailer, remember that the computer world is never without risk. If you require perfection, you'd better stay away from computer software altogether. That said, software obtained over the Internet is no riskier than shrink-wrap software from a retail outlet as long as you remember to take reasonable precautions as described in this chapter.

> ☆ **TIP**   **Macintosh Users Only**
>
> You must check out the *ultimate* Macintosh site at `http://www.ultimatemac.com`. Then drop by `http://maccentral.macworld.com/` for breaking news and new software releases.

If you're still worried and want to stick to popular mainstream software, you can search the Web to find out everything anyone has ever said about the software you're considering. If it has a problem, you're bound to hear about it. Remember, you're plugged in to the world's largest grapevine. Listen to the buzz, use your common sense, and see how long it takes to fill a 60GB hard drive. This is one place where you can have a lot of fun with your computer.

Software Reviews

If you know exactly what you want, it's easy to find it at a large software clearing-house and proceed with the download process. But finding software often involves deciding what you want in the first place. What if you don't even know what software you want? Happily, the Internet has the answer for that, too.

If you want to get serious about making informed software decisions, start by reading reviews. You can try out a demo version of many kinds of software, but you probably don't want to test-drive every car on the lot. By seeing what the reviewers have to say, you should be able to limit your choices or, in some cases, to learn about other solutions that may take you in a different direction altogether. Software reviews are usually educational and sometimes entertaining, but they're almost always time-savers. You can also find comments on message boards and mailing lists, which are good places to ask specific questions if you have them. But if you're just getting into an area where you have little experience, a good software review is the place to start.

As you might expect, there are plenty of software reviews to be found on the Net in newsletters, e-zines, and at large software clearinghouses. Some reviews are archived in sites that specialize in the software industry or in special-interest sites for particular professions. For example, sites for teachers may review educational software, art sites may review graphics editors and drawing programs, and sites for interior designers may review software for house layouts. When you find specialized sites that interest you, it's a good idea to bookmark them.

Meanwhile, here are some places you can visit to find reviews of mainstream software. Note that not all software gets reviewed. Applets and JavaScript scripts for Web pages are not likely to be reviewed by anyone (there are too many of them). And a lot of good freeware and shareware programs never got enough attention to earn a review. As a rule, the best software out there gets noticed, so you might want to avoid any software that hasn't been noticed by someone in a position to write about it. If you install only software that has been reviewed, you are much less likely to be victimized by a malicious bit of code.

All Operating Systems

☆ The Cool Tool Network (`http://www.cooltool.com/search.cgi`)
☆ ZDNet Reviews (`http://www.zdnet.com/products/`)

Windows

☆ Stroud's CWSA Apps (`http://cws.internet.com/`)
☆ Win Planet Reviews (`http://www.winplanet.com/winplanet/subjects/`)
☆ Digital Duck (`http://www.digitalduck.com/`)
☆ Netigen Web (`http://www.netigen.com/reviews.html`)
☆ PCToday.com Supersite (`http://www.pctoday.com/mini/smartcomputing/editorial/reviews.asp?rid=396&guid=wlvapo30`)
☆ PCWORLD.COM Reviews (`http://www.pcworld.com/top400/0,1375,software,00.html`)

Macintosh

☆ MacReview Zone (`http://www.macreviewzone.com/`)
☆ MacDirectory (`http://www.pacifeeder.com/macintosh/software.htm`)
☆ Macs Only (`http://www.macsonly.com/`)
☆ MacHome Journal Online Reviews (`http://database.machome.com/Reviews/reviews.lasso`)

◎◎ Understanding the Download Process

The following is a step-by-step guide to downloading software from the Internet.

Select the Right Software File for Your Computer

In general, different operating systems cannot run the exact same computer programs. Each operating system requires its own set of executable code. Popular software is often available for different platforms, so make sure you are downloading the version that's right for you (see Figure 2.2). If you download the wrong one, you won't be able to install or run it on your computer. Most Web sites make it easy to pick the right version.

Note that many software offerings are available for the PC or the Macintosh, but not both. If the software you want is not available for your computer, look for something similar that's made for your platform.

VirusScan V4.0 for Windows 3.X
$29.95 USD
#1 Virus Detection and Removal
🛈 More Info
🛒 Add to Cart

VirusScan V4.0 for Windows 95/98
$29.95 USD
#1 Virus Detection and Removal
🛈 More Info
🛒 Add to Cart

VirusScan V4.0.3a for Win NT (INTEL)
$29.95 USD
#1 Virus Detection and Removal
🛈 More Info
🛒 Add to Cart

Figure 2.2 Select the Right Software for Your Computer

Most links on Web pages point to other Web pages. But some Web page links point to software files instead of Web pages. When you click on such a link for a software file, it's up to your browser to decide what to do. If your browser doesn't recognize the file type, it will ask you. Browsers recognize software files by their file extensions. The most commonly used extensions for Windows software are `.exe` and `.zip`; for Macintosh, `.bin`, `.sit`, and `.sea`. Browsers can be configured to respond to any file extension, but when no specific instructions have been given, you will be asked whether you want to save the file to your hard drive or open it (see Figure 2.3).

> ☆ **SHORTCUT**   Appendix B describes additional file extensions that you may encounter.

> ☆ **TIP**   **Macintosh Files and File Extensions**
>
> Macintosh computers are configured to display filenames without their file extensions. As a result, a file that you download to a Mac may appear with a file extension on the browser screen but show up without that file extension on the Macintosh. This is just a display discrepancy. It's still the same file.

Always Save to File or Save to Disk

When your browser encounters a file that is not an HTML file or an image file, it checks a list of known file extensions; it can then open recognized file types using software already available on your computer. This is a good idea for data files such as `.pdf` or `.mp3` files, but it's not a good idea for executable files, which should be scanned for viruses before you execute them. So you should configure your browser to let you choose what to do when executable files are encountered. *If you're asked what to do with an executable file, always elect to save it to a file.* This will let you scan the file for viruses before it gets executed.

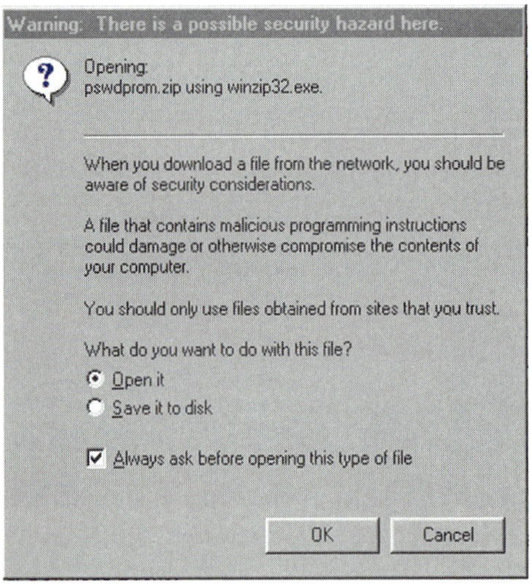

Figure 2.3 The Safest Option Is Save It to Disk

☆ **TIP**   **Which Files Are Executable?**

There are hundreds of file extensions and few people know them all. If you aren't sure about a file extension, assume it's executable. It's always better to be safe than sorry.

☆ **WARNING** **Stay in Charge**

Sometimes it's best not to delegate decisions to your Web browser. If you ever see a check box that says "Always ask before opening this type of file," make sure you keep that box checked. This is a safeguard against hackers and malicious code.

Check your browser's preference settings before you download executable files so that you can make sure the browser is not set to automatically execute any file before you've scanned it. Preference settings can be reset without your knowledge (especially if other people have access to your computer). If you're ever given an option to turn off a pop-up window that gives you control over a file download, don't turn it off.

> ⭐ **WARNING** **Firewalls**
>
> Computers in university computer labs, public libraries, and workplaces are often configured to prevent unauthorized software installations. Organizations often use a special program called a **firewall** that monitors and controls all file transfers from the Internet. If you use a computer that doesn't permit you to download software files from the Internet, you cannot install software from the Internet. You'll need to use your own personal computer.

Similarly, you may be given a choice between saving the program to disk or running the program from its current location (see Figure 2.4). Again, the safest option is to save the program to disk. By the way, you can't run the program from its current location on the server; you're really downloading it to a temporary location on your computer, where it will then be executed. If you know and trust the file in question (because you've downloaded and scanned it before), running from its current location may save you from having to delete a temporary executable later. But most of the time, you shouldn't trust the file, and you should opt to save it to a location of your choice. This practice will ensure that you have a chance to scan the file for viruses if your virus scanner must be manually launched.

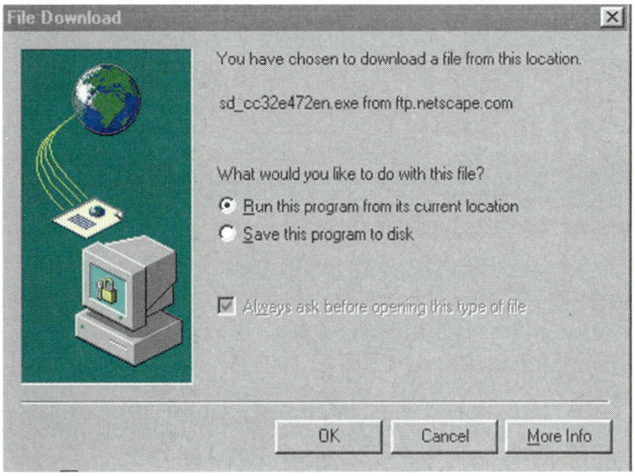

Figure 2.4 The Safest Option Is "Save this program to disk"

After you select Save to File, you select a location on your hard drive for the new file. You can either accept the default location suggested by your browser or select a different location on your hard drive. It doesn't matter where you put the file as long as you know where it's going (you'll need to find it later).

Put All Your File Downloads into a Special Folder

Your browser will suggest a location for your file downloads based on its preference settings. As just mentioned, you can override this default location, but it's easier to remember the location if you always put your downloads in the same place. Then you'll always know where to find them after the download is complete.

> ☆**TIP**   If you accidentally download a file to an unknown folder, you can find it by searching your hard drive using Windows Explorer or a similar **file manager** program. You must have the filename, so if you've forgotten it you may have to return to the download site.

As soon as you select a location for your file, the download will begin. Your browser will show you how it's going. Figure 2.5 shows how Netscape Navigator tracks its file downloads. Internet Explorer has its own download manager, which can start and track multiple downloads simultaneously. Although it's useful to see this progress report for a large download, you don't have to drop everything to watch it. You can run other applications, including your browser, while the download continues in the background. Just don't drop your Internet connection until the download is over.

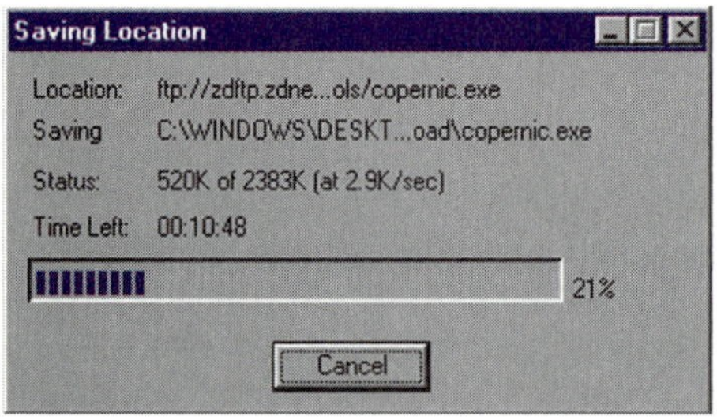

Figure 2.5 Netscape Navigator's Download Progress Report

Scan for Viruses Right after the Download

When the download is over, the file will be stored on your hard drive. Now is the time to scan the file for viruses. Assuming you have virus protection software on your computer, make sure you understand how it operates. Some virus detection utilities can be configured to automatically scan all new files as soon as they appear on your hard drive. Others must be run manually. Figure 2.6 shows how McAfee VirusScan can be invoked to check all the files currently found in a folder on the desktop, including the most recent download, copernic.exe. *Do not run any executable file until it has been checked out by your virus protection software.*

Note that you cannot be infected with a computer virus if all you do is download an infected file. You must *execute* a file in order to activate a virus. A virus scanner that automatically intercepts and scans all new files coming onto your hard drive will protect you in case you forget to do it yourself. Just make sure that your virus scanner is running in the background whenever you download executables from the Internet. After the file has been scanned and deemed safe to open, you can install the software.

> ☆**WARNING** **Keep Your Antivirus Software Up-to-Date**
>
> All virus scanners rely on data files that contain descriptions of known viruses. These files must be updated periodically. If your computer came with an antivirus program and you've never updated its virus files, your computer is vulnerable to new computer viruses. To find out how to update your virus files, visit the home page of your antivirus software.

Understanding the Download Process

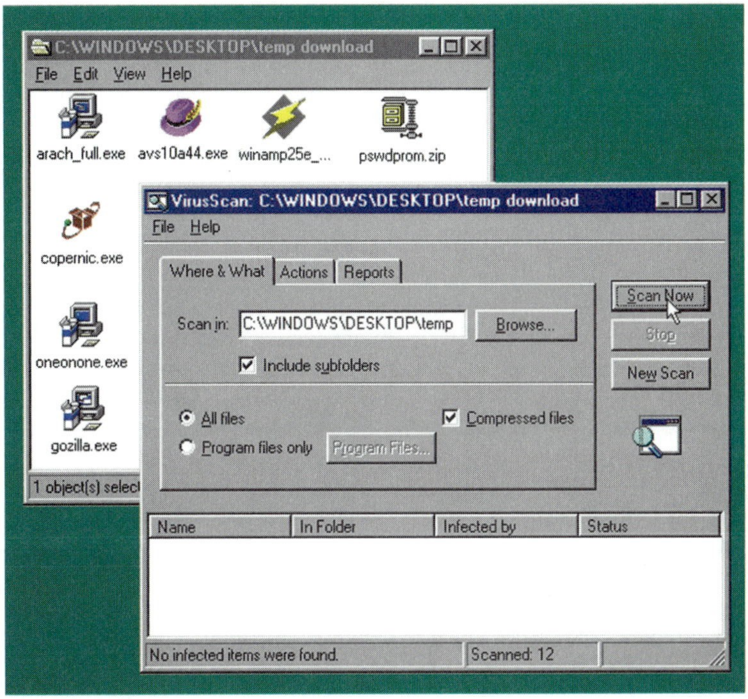

Figure 2.6 Scan the Download for Viruses Before You Open It

Software that is configured to automatically open executable files is responsible for the spread of many computer viruses. For example, any e-mail program that automatically opens attachments is extremely dangerous (although people who indiscriminately open e-mail attachments are just as dangerous). Many e-mail viruses are spread by Microsoft Outlook and Outlook Express because these mail programs launch executable scripts inside mail messages. People using other mail programs will not be affected when they receive infected mail messages. Similarly, Microsoft Word spreads **macro viruses** (executable code that can be launched when Word opens an infected Word document) unless Word's preference setting for automatic macro execution is disabled.

In short, you should treat all executable files or files containing executable components with extreme caution.

◎◎ Installing Downloaded Software

Software installation is usually simple, but you can encounter a few stumbling blocks if you're inexperienced and don't know what to expect. This section describes the standard scenarios so that you can install software from the Internet without fear.

There are four basic installation scenarios:

★ Executable installers (most commonly used for large commercial programs)

★ Ready-to-go executables (most commonly used for smaller, noncommercial programs)

★ Zipped file archives (most commonly used for smaller, noncommercial programs)

★ ActiveX installers (requires Internet Explorer on a Windows system)

We will discuss each of these in turn. Note that the file extensions for Windows are different from those on a Macintosh, but the general installation steps are the same for either platform. The Web site where you find your download will not bother to explain which installation scenario applies, but with a little experience you will come to recognize the different installation scenarios and the usual procedures associated with them.

Executable Installers

If your download is an `.exe` file (`.sea` for a Mac), you have probably downloaded an **installer**. If the file's icon includes an arrow pointing downward or a picture of a box and a floppy in front of a computer, you're definitely looking at an installer file. An installer is used for programs that require multiple files. These might include one file for the actual executable code, additional data files (such as help files), and graphics files (for animations or ad banners). To install these files manually, you would need to follow detailed instructions about where to save the various files, and you would probably have to edit at least a few of the files. Because manual installations are time-consuming and prone to error, it's much better to bundle complex software inside an installer that can do all the busywork for you.

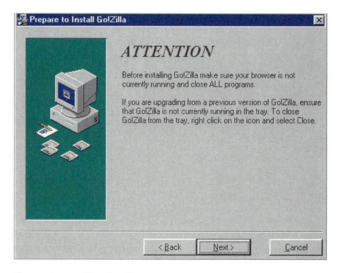

Figure 2.7 Read and Follow the Installer's Instructions

Figure 2.7 shows the first screen of an installer for a Windows program named Go!Zilla. If you download a lot of software, you will see the same installers used over and over. Each installer has its own look, but they all ask the same sorts of questions and do the same sorts of things.

You execute an installer only once. Then you can discard it or save it in case you ever need to reinstall the software. Some people like to save their installers so that they can re-create their computing environment when they upgrade to a new computer. If you have plenty of space on your hard drive, you might want to save all your installers in a special folder. Zip disks and super drive disks are especially useful for saving installers if you don't want to eat up memory on your hard drive.

☆ **WARNING** **Close Other Applications**

Most installers remind you to shut down other programs before proceeding. In some cases, your new software will not run properly if you try to install it while other programs are running. In many cases, an installer cannot execute properly while a virus scanner is running in the background. It is safe to turn off the virus scanner during installation as long as you remember to turn it back on afterward.

☆ **TIP** **When to Turn Off Your Virus Protection Software**

Sometimes a software installer will ask you to turn off your virus protection software before you begin the installation. This may sound suspicious, but it can be a perfectly legitimate requirement. If an installer asks you to turn off your scanner, you should do it (or abort the installation). Turning off your scanner does entail some risk. Don't install software that asks you to turn off your scanner unless the software is popular and well known.

Most installers will ask you a few questions, giving you control of certain aspects of the installation. Typically, the first question asks where you want to put the executable file(s). The installer suggests a location, but you can override it if you prefer to put the program in a different folder. Remember that Windows shortcuts and Mac aliases let you access a program from various locations, so the folder where it's stored may not be important. If you have no reason to care, take the installer's suggestion and don't worry about it.

Although it doesn't matter where you put a program, once you've installed it, don't move any of the program's files. If you ever need to move a software installation to another directory for any reason, you should uninstall the software and reinstall it again from scratch.

The installer may ask additional questions. The more complicated the software, the more questions may be asked. Although installers generally try to explain themselves when they ask you for input, you may not be sure how to answer a question. For example, you might be asked whether you want a standard installation or a custom installation. In this case, the standard installation will be the installer's default setting, but you can opt for a custom install if you understand the software well enough to take more control over the installation process (custom installations always involve more questions). If you don't understand a question, read any help files that the installer may offer and try to make sense out of the question as best you can. If you still don't understand a question, it's best to go with the choice suggested by the installer. Don't worry. The default setting is almost always the right one.

Installers usually display the software's license agreement and refuse to complete the installation if you do not agree to the terms. If you click I Agree, you have entered into a legally binding contract. As discussed in Chapter One, it's a good idea to read the license agreement just as you read any contract before you sign it.

> **★TIP   Read Everything the Installer Has to Say**
>
> Most installations are short and sweet. But if an installer gives you something to read, it's wise to read it. It may alert you to potential software conflicts, useful features, and other important information (see Figure 2.8).

You may also find important information about software incompatibilities buried in these agreements. When you add new software to your computer, you should find out everything you can about it. Computer programs often depend on shared resources. This means that two computer programs can interact with each other in unexpected ways even if they aren't running at the same time. As a result, you may find that your system crashes a lot after you've installed a new program even if the new program isn't running at the time of the crash.

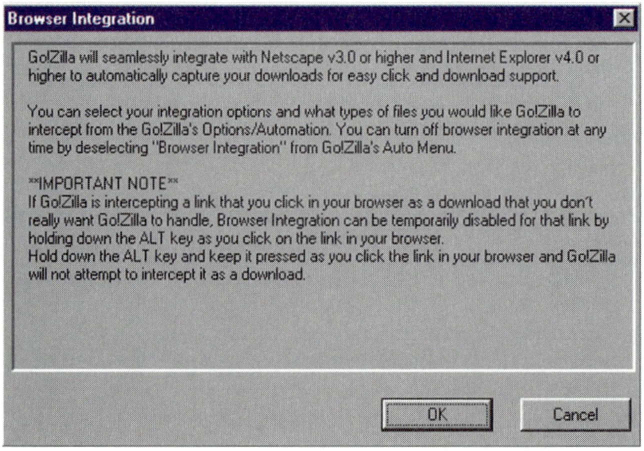

Figure 2.8 Some Installers Contain Important Information

Sometimes a separate README file is packed with the software. This file contains last-minute information about problems and how to avoid them. If you have a problem with your software, always check the README file before contacting the manufacturer for assistance. You can solve many problems this way.

The final screen informs you that the installation is complete. At that point, you may be given an opportunity to examine a README file, or you may be invited to run the application for the first time. Either way, your software is in place and ready to launch.

> ☆ **TIP**   **Always Read the README File**
>
> README files are a software tradition. When a program's author (or manufacturer) discovers a prob-
> lem with the program, it's often reported in the README file. In that way, anyone who grabs the
> most recent version of the software will be up-to-date on all the known problems and possible fixes.
> Of course, this works only when everyone downloading the software bothers to read the README
> file. It's a good system, but you have to do your part and read the README.

Some installers automatically place a shortcut to the application on your desktop (this practice is more common on PCs than Macs). You can delete the shortcut
if you don't want it. Some installers also add the application to your Start menu
(another PC tradition). Both practices are designed to make it easy for you to find
your new application. If you opt out of these conveniences, you can still run the
program as long as you know where it's located on your hard drive (remember
when the installer asked you where to save the program?). If you can't remember,
you can run a search for a file with the name of the application, or possibly any
file with a recent creation date. As long as you know that a program is on your
computer, you should be able to find it. The more common problem is forgetting
that it's there.

Ready-to-Go Executables

If a computer program is simple enough, the entire program can be stored in a single file and doesn't require an involved installation process. With these **ready-to-
go executables**, you download the executable file, which you can run as soon as
it arrives. You need only decide where you want to store the program file. It doesn't
matter where you put it, and you can move it if you want to. Unlike more complicated programs, you don't have to uninstall and reinstall this kind of software.

A ready-to-go executable won't have a README file, so be sure to check the
author's Web site for recent news and announcements. If you need help operating
the software or setting its user preferences, check the program for a Help menu. If
that doesn't do the trick, check the author's Web site for additional documentation. Programmers who distribute their own programs over the Web often rely on
the Web as their primary means of communication. So if the program does not
include much documentation, check for a URL instead. You may find all sorts of
useful resources on the author's Web site, such as a user manual, the most recent
README file, and other timely communications.

A ready-to-go executable is usually an `.exe` file (for Windows) or a `.bin` file
(for the Macintosh). Sometimes you may see an ASCII-encoded executable (`.uue`
for Unix and Windows or `.hqx` for the Mac), although these older formats are
much less common.

Zipped File Archives

Multiple software files are often compressed and packed into archives for convenient downloading (it's easier to download a single archive file than 10 or 100 separate software files). A `.zip` extension (Windows) or a `.sit` extension (Mac)
normally signals a file archive. File archives are easy to unpack but they require a

file utility. For more on file archives, see File Utilities and File Archives later in this chapter.

As soon as you can see what's inside the archive, look for a README file (see Figure 2.9). It will tell you what to do next.

☆ **SHORTCUT**   You may encounter a **self-extracting archive** (usually an .exe file for Windows or .sea for Macs) which unpacks itself automatically when you doubleclick on it. For this reason, it's always a good idea to isolate any .exe or .sea file in a new file folder before you doubleclick. Self-extracting archives "explode" and deposit all their contents into the current directory. You don't want 100 files exploding onto your desktop or some other important folder containing unrelated files. If you later decide to delete the archive, it's a simple matter to delete a special-purpose folder. It's much harder to sift through a large number of files, some archive files and some not, trying to figure out which ones are safe to delete.

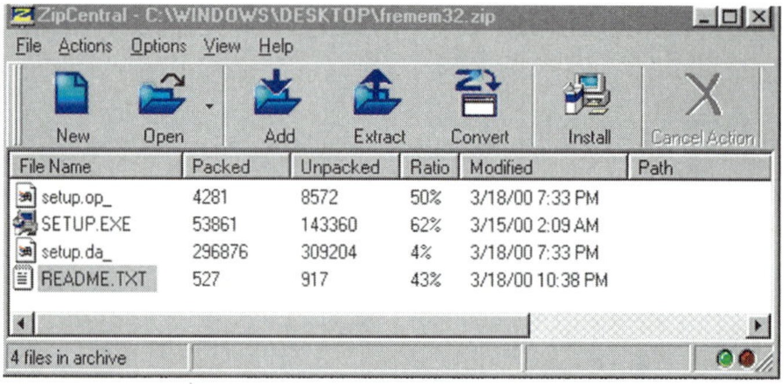

Figure 2.9 A File Archive Named "fremem32.zip"

Some file archives contain a ready-to-go executable along with documenation files. Others contain an installer instead of a ready-to-go executable. You have to read the README file in order to know what's going on.

In the case of Freemem Professional, a file named "setup.exe" is an installer file. The README file explains what you need to know before you run this particular installer (see Figure 2.10). Each README file contains different instructions so it is a good idea to look for the README file and read it carefully before proceeding with the software installation.

ActiveX Installers

Another software installation scenario relies on **ActiveX controls**, which are distributed with Internet Explorer (versions 3.0 and higher). The idea behind ActiveX installations is to make software downloads and installations as simple as possible. You click on a certain link, and you're finished.

McAfee's Virus Clinic is an example of a software installation that relies on ActiveX. You can download Virus Clinic using a browser other than Internet Explorer through the use of an ActiveX plug-in (see Chapter Three for an introduction to plug-ins), but you must have Internet Explorer installed on your system for the plug-in to work.

```
Readme.txt - Notepad                    _ □ ×
File  Edit  Search  Help

FreeMem Professional Version 4.3
for Microsoft Windows.

BEFORE INSTALLING Version 4, make sure that
you close any running copy of FreeMem Professional.

If you have any older version of FreeMem
Professional running, please install into
the same folder.

This program enables you to stay in control
of Windows memory management. It is possible
to free up a specified amount of RAM. This will
make working with your PC a lot smoother. You
can verify the result with the integrated easy
to understand statistics. Unattended regular
operations and special boot-time options are
easily set up. A tray icon or a window on the
taskbar will keep you informed on your memory
status.

New for Version 4.3:
* Compatibility with Microsoft Windows 2000
* A 'Defaults' button for easy setup

To install this program, just run setup.exe

Meikel Weber
meikel@Meikel.com
http://www.meikel.com/
```

Figure 2.10 This README File Explains How to Install Freemem Professional

One problem with ActiveX controls is that a malicious one can be programmed to do anything. Unlike programs written with other Web languages (such as JavaScript and Java), which restrict what their programs can do to preserve system security, ActiveX controls have no such restrictions. ActiveX controls can create and remove files on your hard drive and run executable files. They can search for personal information in data files for applications such as Quicken and send those files onto the Internet without your permission. They can hunt down your e-mail address and ship it to countless spamming operations. They can steal your credit card information and passwords to restricted Web sites if you store them on your computer without encryption. Moreover, an ActiveX installer can be programmed to execute malicious code at some future date, making it impossible to connect the destructive code with its source on the Web. The destructive potential of malicious ActiveX controls is unlimited if steps are not taken to protect the innocent.

This means that you must be very careful with ActiveX installations. You must trust the site that uses an ActiveX installer, and you must make sure that the sponsors of the site are really who they say they are. If a deceptive Web site tricks you into running a malicious ActiveX installer, the potential for destruction is great.

You cannot scan ActiveX programs for viruses because these programs execute automatically after downloading. This makes ActiveX downloads risky because you must take someone else's word for it that the program is safe to execute. Microsoft understands the risks inherent in ActiveX and has taken steps to protect consumers from malicious ActiveX downloads. A mechanism called Authenticode enables a system developer (such as Microsoft) to place a digital certificate on any ActiveX control that it has created. A **digital certificate** is like a digital ID card that your browser can examine and verify. Whenever your browser encounters a digital certificate, it will check the certificate to make sure it is legitimate before going ahead with the download. If your browser sees a certificate it can't verify, it will issue a warning (see Figure 2.11). For more information about ActiveX security issues, visit `http://www.microsoft.com/security/new.asp`.

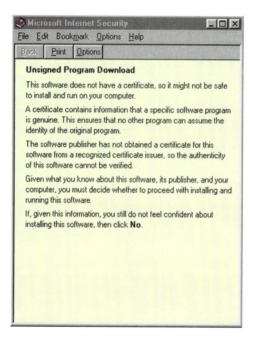

Figure 2.11 Digital Certificates Can Protect You from Malicious ActiveX Installations

A certificate verification failure may or may not mean that the software in question is risky. But if you want to be as safe as possible, reject any software that cannot be authenticated by your browser.

The display in Figure 2.12 warns about a program file that does not contain an Authenticode signature. This means that its authorship cannot be verified. Judging from the URL, the file appears to be coming from Microsoft's own Web site, but someone could have broken into the server and planted malicious code. If you ever see something like this and you want to play it safe, contact the distributor (in this case Microsoft) before accepting the download.

Critics of the Authenticode system point out that a verified signature is only as good as its source. If you trust the source to distribute software that does what it says it does and nothing more, a digital signature will give you peace of mind.

Unfortunately, some software manufacturers embed functionality in their software that they consider benign but that you might disapprove of (if you knew what it was doing).

Figure 2.12 You Can't Be Sure Where This Unsigned File Came From

For example, in 1999, millions of people downloaded the popular freeware version of RealPlayer 7.0, a streaming audio player. Few people who installed RealPlayer bothered to wonder what the Comet Cursor was, although it was listed as a feature in two of three download options (see Figure 2.13).

Select your Free RealPlayer 7 Basic
Based on your connection speed, we have selected a download size for you. To change your selection, check the button next to the one you want.

Features Include:	Complete (7.4 MB)	Standard (7.0 MB)	Minimal (3.4 MB)
Plays all Real content	✓	✓	✓
NEW! Take5 showcase	✓	✓	✓
NEW! Over 100 Radio Stations	✓	✓	✓
Support for MP3	✓	✓	✓
AutoUpdate	✓	✓	✓
Built-in Help	✓	✓	
RealJukebox Basic	✓	✓	
Comet Cursor	✓	✓	
Additional Playback Formats	All	Some	
Est. download time (56k)	18 min.	17 min.	8 min.
Make Your Selection	○	◉	○
Download FREE RealPlayer 7 Basic beta			

Figure 2.13 The Comet Cursor Bundled with RealPlayer

Even if users had taken the time to track down the Comet Systems site (at `http://www.cometsystems.com/`), they wouldn't have found out that this cursor application was tracking user browsing behavior and sending this information to Comet Systems for inclusion in a Web tracking database. Comet Systems neglected to inform its consumers about this aspect of the Comet Cursor until a reporter broke the story, raised questions about online privacy, and forced Comet Systems to explain what it was doing. In this case, a digital signature check for RealPlayer would have made no difference because RealPlayer and Comet Systems chose to distribute software without fully disclosing exactly what it was doing. It's conceivable that the folks at RealPlayer didn't fully understand the capabilities of the Comet Cursor. Would you trust them more or less if they claimed ignorance?

> ☆**TIP**   **Protect Your Privacy**
>
> An **ET application** (named after the extraterrestrial character in the movie "ET") collects data about something you do with your computer and then uses your active Internet connection to send that information to a server that builds a database of user profiles. You can experiment with software downloads without sacrificing your privacy, but you'll need to install a personal firewall to do it. A **personal firewall** monitors all the information that flows between your computer and the Internet and alerts you if any unauthorized communications are attempted. A personal firewall will detect any ET application and shut it down unless you give it permission to phone home. ZoneAlarm is a popular freeware firewall for Windows users.

Trusting your system security to a commercial software manufacturer is a risky business, no matter how much you may like its products. Even Microsoft has been sabotaged by its own programmers (to find out more, do a Web search with the keywords "Microsoft security risk FrontPage98 extensions"), demonstrating that malicious programmers can make mischief anywhere.

If you're concerned about the security risks associated with ActiveX, disable ActiveX (see Online References at the end of this chapter), and simply avoid all software that requires ActiveX. Alternatively, trade in your PC for a Mac. If you aren't sure how much to worry about all this, it may help to remember that even though many things are possible on the Internet, very few worst-case scenarios actually materialize. Moreover, the chances of one happening to you is probably less than the chance of being struck by lightning. In any case, a few simple commonsense precautions are always advisable and can save you from disaster if you should happen to be unlucky:

☆ Back up your entire hard drive or at least the most important files (disastrous hardware failures can happen without warning).

☆ Encrypt your most sensitive data files or store them offline.

☆ Don't download software from questionable places.

Over time, we'll see more variations on software installations, including ASP (Application Service Provider) installations, which minimize the need for full application downloads. And although there are security concerns with tools like ActiveX, these tools can be used to good advantage. So far, the benefits appear to outweigh the risks.

◎◎ File Utilities and File Archives

If you expect to download much software from the Internet, sooner or later you'll need to open a file archive. A **file archive** is a special type of file that contains other files. It's like a file folder. If you have the right file utility program, you can open the archive to see what's inside. If you don't have the right utility, you can't do anything with a file archive.

A `.zip` file extension is used for file archives under Windows. On a Mac, it is almost always a `.sit` file extension. If your system has the appropriate file utility associated with the archive's file extension, you can open an archive by double-clicking it. There are many file utilities that can do the job, but you need only one on hand.

WinZip (Windows shareware) http://www.winzip.com/tucows/

If you're running Windows, the most popular archive utility is WinZip. WinZip is shareware. You can try it for free during a 30-day trial period; then if you use it after 30 days, you must register it (currently, it costs $29). WinZip has won numerous software awards, including ZDNet's "Download of the Millenium."

☆**WARNING** Don't confuse WinZip with the WinZip Self-Extractor, which sells for $49. You don't need the Self-Extractor unless you want to distribute your own software over the Internet.

The WinZip Web site contains excellent documentation, including detailed instructions on how to configure WinZip to launch your virus scanner (conduct a site search using the keyword "virus").

ZipCentral (Windows freeware) http://zipcentral.iscool.net/

Although it's hard to beat WinZip, ZipCentral comes close, and it's freeware. The ZipCentral home page is a little flaky (it's free Web space from Xoom.com), and you may need Internet Explorer to view it correctly. But don't let that scare you away. ZipCentral is robust, easy to use, and filled with the most important features found in WinZip. You won't get the same tech support that you get with WinZip, but chances are you won't need it, so that shouldn't be a serious concern. If you have trouble configuring ZipCentral to launch your virus scanner, visit the WinZip Web site and check out its documentation on virus scanners. The same information applies to ZipCentral.

Stuffit Expander (Macintosh freeware) http://www.aladdinsys.com/expander/expander_mac_login.html

This is a must-have freeware utility for all Macintosh owners. Do not confuse Stuffit Expander with Stuffit Deluxe, which sells for $79.95, or Stuffit Lite, which sells for $30. You don't need Stuffit Deluxe or Stuffit Lite unless you want to distribute your own software over the Internet.

Using Your File Utility

If you download one of the utilities mentioned here, you can handle any software file types.

> ☆ **TIP**   You'd be in trouble if you need-
> ed a file utility to unpack a newly down-
> loaded file utility. Happily, the people who
> distribute file utilities understand this, so
> they're careful to give you installers or
> ready-to-go executables when you down-
> load their utilities.

Using a Download Manager

If your Internet connection tends to die on you in the middle of long downloads, you'll find that a download manager will improve your quality of life. **Download managers** are utilities that specialize in file downloads and offer many features not found in Web browsers. Web browsers handle file downloads in a basic way, but a download manager handles file downloads in style. You'll learn about download managers in more detail in Chapter Three.

Uninstalling Software

When you experiment with software downloads, you're bound to regret an installation from time to time. A program may not be what you thought it was. It may be missing an important feature, the documentation may be too sketchy, or it may cause software conflicts. Then it's time to **uninstall** the software. Uninstalling a program removes from your hard drive all files associated with the original installation.

Some software is easier to uninstall than others. It depends on your operating system and the specific piece of software.

In the easiest case, the software comes with its own uninstaller, which you'll find in the same directory (folder) that holds the software's main executable file. Some people refuse to install new software unless it features an uninstaller. In Windows, you should be able to see available software uninstallers from the Start menu (look under Programs). All you do is run the uninstaller.

Windows also helps you remove unwanted software with its own installation monitor. To uninstall a program, follow these steps.

1. Quit (close) all running applications.

2. From the Start menu, choose Settings, and then choose Control Panel.

3. Double-click the icon labeled Add/Remove Programs.

4. Make sure you are looking at the Install/Uninstall tab.

5. Look for the software you want to remove in the scrollable text window.

6. Highlight the title you want to remove, and click the Add/Remove button.

7. Click Yes.

> ☆ **TIP**   **For Windows ME and XP Users**
>
> If you're running Windows Millenium Edition or Windows XP, you have System Restore, a feature that lets you create a **system checkpoint** before you add any new software to your computer. If you later decide you don't like the installation, you can return your operating system to its exact state at the saved checkpoint. System checkpoints can be used to back up important OS files that are changed by software installations, but they do not give you a complete system backup (you cannot recover all files as they existed at the time of the checkpoint). To create a system checkpoint, click the Start button, and choose Programs ➔ Accessories ➔ System Tools ➔ System Restore.

This method may not return your operating system to exactly the state it was in before the software installation, but the remaining persistent effects are small and usually of no consequence.

On a Macintosh, you usually have to visit a few folders to look for application-specific files that you can delete manually. These files are found in the following:

⭐ The application folder itself (somewhere on your hard drive)

⭐ The Control Panels folder (inside the System folder)

⭐ The Extensions folder (inside the System folder)

⭐ The Preferences folder (inside the System folder)

⭐ **TIP**　　**Uninstalling Internet Explorer**

It's difficult, if not impossible, to uninstall the Internet Explorer Web browser under Windows. Microsoft says that IE is an integral part of the Windows operating system (at the time of this writing, Microsoft is fighting an antitrust suit over this issue). If you're curious, conduct a general Web search with the search query "uninstalling Internet Explorer" for more information.

◎◎ Computer Viruses and AntiVirus Software

A **computer virus** is a program that surreptitiously spreads from one computer to another. Some viruses do a lot of damage to the machines they infect, and others are barely noticeable. An extremely destructive virus could erase every file on your hard drive. Most viruses are written by young people who may or may not understand the full consequences of their actions. A variety of laws make it illegal to harm computers with malicious software, but it is difficult to apprehend the perpetrators of these crimes, and hundreds of viruses have been making the rounds for years.

The Internet makes it easy to spread viruses to computers whose owners are not cautious and vigilant. More than 90 percent of home computers run Windows, and most computer viruses are designed to attack Windows computers. Fewer viruses are aimed at Macs, although Macintosh viruses can be just as devastating.

Viruses are spread whenever an executable file containing a virus is moved from one computer to another computer. Because computer programs are executable files, you have to worry about computer viruses whenever you download software from the Internet. *If you do not have up-to-date virus protection software running on your computer, you should not download software from the Internet.*

Let's assume that you want to minimize your risk and you have obtained virus protection for your computer. Now you need to investigate its configuration so that you will understand how it works. Some virus protection software must be run manually on individual files or file folders whenever you want to scan for viruses. Other packages can be set to run in the background, where they intercept all incoming files and scan them automatically. The latter type is especially convenient for people who do a lot of software downloads; this protection mode will keep you safe even if you forget to scan an incoming file from a download site.

Running Your Scanner in the Background

If you rely on a virus scanner that runs in the background, always double-check to make sure it is really running before you begin a software installation. It's wonderful to have a background scanner so that you don't have to run manual scans. But a background scanner must be active in order to work. It's easy to forget about a background scanner because it doesn't bother to tell you when a scan turns up nothing; scanners make their presence known only when they detect a virus.

Whether your software is set up to intercept incoming files automatically or to scan on manual command, you also need to check your preference settings to make sure that the scanner is set to check all incoming files and not just executable files (see Figure 2.14).

Note that some scanners can be configured to open file archives and scan their contents. Others cannot scan the contents of a file archive unless you open the archive. However, all scanners will check any files being copied onto your hard drive, and this includes files being extracted from a file archive (as well as files created by a software installer). So even if no virus warning is triggered when you download a software file archive, you may get a warning when files are being extracted from an archive. One way or another, your virus scanner will protect you when you download file archives (as long as you have it turned on).

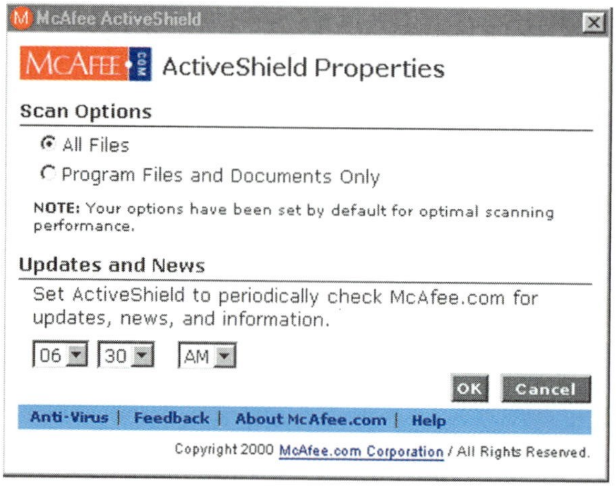

Figure 2.14 Check Your Scanner's Preference Settings

It never hurts to have your scanner configured to test as many incoming files as possible. The CPU load is negligible, and you always need to worry about macro viruses.

Most virus scanners allow you to scan specific files or folders on demand. If you have one that does, check to see whether you can configure your file archive utility to launch your virus scanner from inside the archive program. In Figure 2.15, for example, ZipCentral is being configured to find a virus scanner, and Figure 2.16 shows how to launch a virus scanner from inside ZipCentral.

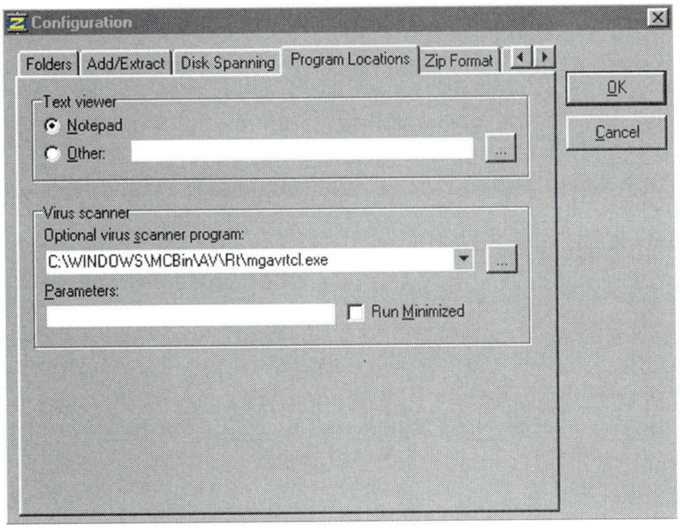

Figure 2.15 ZipCentral Has a Preference Setting for Your Virus Scanner

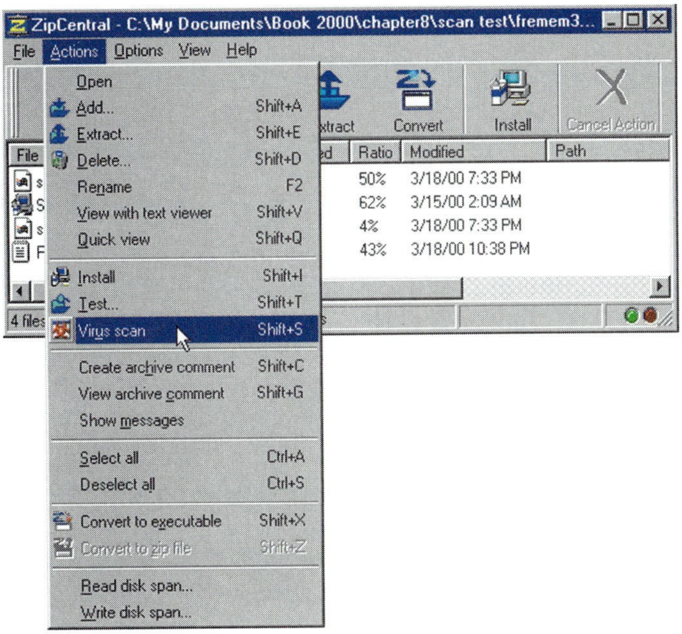

Figure 2.16 Scanning a File inside a File Archive Before You Extract It

When you can plug your virus scanner into your archive utility, you can manually scan the archived files before they are extracted. This isn't really necessary if your scanner is running in the background, ready to pounce on any infected files as soon as they're extracted from the archive. But some people like to be reassured by scanning file archives manually before they proceed with an installation. A scanner running in the background doesn't tell you that no viruses are found; it alerts you only when a virus is found. A manual file scan always reports its results whether or not a virus is found. It never hurts to run both an automatic scan and a manual scan on the same files.

☆ Summary

▶ Never download software from obscure Web sites. Instead, use popular software clearinghouses and Web sites for reputable software manufacturers.

▶ Downloading software means copying software files from a server onto your hard drive. Software installation is a separate step (except with ActiveX).

▶ All software installations follow standard procedures, depending on what you have: an executable installer, a ready-to-go executable, a zipped file archive, a self-extracting archive, or an ActiveX installer.

▶ To unpack a file archive, you'll need a file archive utility.

▶ Computer viruses are activated only when you execute an executable file; you cannot trigger a virus by merely copying a file on to your hard drive. Scan all new files with antivirus software, and keep your antivirus software up-to-date.

☆ Online References

Downloading Software from the Internet: PC TechPaper Tutorial for Beginners.
http://www.siliconguide.com/internet/download/download.shtml

Downloading Software for the Mac.
http://cybered.umassd.edu/public/CyberEdHelp/tutorial/downMAC.html

Downloading Software and Files: It's Easier Than You Think
http://www.rmlibrary.com/news/news03.htm

ZDNet Help & How To: How To Protect Against Computer Viruses.
http://www.zdnet.com/zdhelp/stories/main/0,5594,2248291,00.html

An Overview of Computer Viruses and Antivirus Software.
http://www.hicom.net/~oedipus/virus32.html

Preventing Possible Web Intrusions:Learn To Disable ActiveX, Java & JavaScript
http://www.smartcomputing.com/editorial/article.asp?article=articles%2Farchive%2Fg0804%2F37g04%2F37g04%2Easp

☆ Review Questions

1. Explain why it's important to check for platform compatibility when you download software from the Internet.

2. Suppose you download an executable file that contains a virus. Can you catch the virus by simply downloading the file? Why or why not?

41

3. When you're downloading an executable file, you might be asked whether you want to run the file "from its current location." What does that really mean? Should you do it? Can you think of a circumstance when this option might be preferable? Explain your answer.

4. What does it mean to have a virus scanner running in the background? Why is this a good idea?

5. What is an installer, and when does it make sense to package a computer program inside an installer? How often do you have to run the same installer? Why might you want to save an installer after you've used it to install a program?

6. What do you need on your computer in order to install software with an ActiveX installer?

7. Web browsers can be configured to open certain files for you automatically. When is it appropriate for a browser to do this, and when is it inappropriate? Explain your answer.

8. At what point during a software installation does the licensing agreement become legally binding?

9. What should you always do before you begin a software installation?

10. What is an uninstaller, and where do you get one?

☆ Hands-On Exercises

1. For Windows users only. A graphics utility called Eyedropper can be found at `http://eyedropper.inetia.com/HTML/eng/default.asp`, where it is distributed as a zipped file archive. If you are working on a PC, visit this site and download the latest version of EyeDropper. Scan your download for viruses, and then install the software. Did you have any difficulties with the installation? How many files were inside the zip archive? What were their names? Use your new program to find the hexadecimal color codes for the Vizija logo at the bottom of the download page. The logo contains blue and brown. Find the color codes for those two colors. How long did it take you to complete this exercise?

2. For Mac users only. The EyeDropper program described in Exercise 1 does not run on a Mac, but there are similar programs for Mac users. Go to `http://www.tucows.com` and conduct a search using the keyword "ColorFinder." This will take you to a freeware utility for the Mac. The download for this file is an `.hqx` file, which can be opened with Stuffit Expander. Scan your download for viruses, and then install the software. Did you have any difficulties with the installation? How many files were inside the archive? What were their names? Use your new program to find the hexadecimal color codes for the bird at the top of `http://www-edlab.cs.umass.edu/cs120/index01.html`. The bird has a yellow beak and orange feet.

Find the color codes for those two colors. How long did it take you to complete this exercise?

3. For Windows users only. Go to `http://pluto.spaceports.com/~mobysw/en/mailto-encrypter.html` and download MailTo-Encrypter 1.1. This tool is used to foil **spambots**, which harvest e-mail addresses from Web pages. What does this program do? Scan the download for viruses and then install. Is this download an installer or a ready-to-go executable? How does MailTo-Encrypter encrypt the address `lehnert@cs.umass.edu`?

4. The MP3 file format is used to store audio files on the Internet, but if you want to burn an audio CD, you must first convert your MP3 files to WAV files. Programs that convert from MP3 format to WAV format are called **rippers**. Visit some software clearinghouses and see if you can find any freeware rippers. Can you find one for Windows and another one for the Mac? Which are the most popular choices for each platform? Hint: To find the most popular freeware ripper for Windows, go to CNet's download site (`download.cnet.com`) and navigate the subject tree starting from Audio → Rippers & Encoders. Re-sort the list of software titles to see the most popular downloads by clicking on the Downloads header at the top of the results list.

5. Find out how many Web browsers are available for Windows 95 and Windows 98 by visiting the software clearinghouse at `http://www.dave-central.com/`. Go to the Windows part of the archive, click on the index category Web Surfing, and then go to Browsers.

CHAPTER THREE

CUSTOMIZING YOUR ONLINE EXPERIENCE

As you become more familiar with your computing needs, you'll want to refine and customize your computing environment to be more in tune with your personal work routines. In this chapter you'll learn about software that's especially useful for supporting your work online. Some of these utilities may be valuable to you, and others may not be. Only you can decide what you need to make you more productive online.

◎◎ Chapter Objectives

★ To explore browser customizations with plug-ins, add-ons, and helper applications

★ To discover the convenience of download managers

★ To learn how a password manager helps you handle your Web site sign-ins

★ To see how to use cookie managers and ad filters to protect your privacy

◎◎ Plug-Ins, Add-Ons, and Helper Applications

Application programs are the pieces of software you choose to run on your computer. (That's in contrast to **system software**, which is what your computer uses to run its own operations.) Your chosen applications make your computer unique and personal (hence the name "personal computer"). A Web browser is just another application, and your browser may support additional built-in applications. For example, Internet Explorer and Netscape Navigator have a built-in **Java Virtual Machine** (JVM) so that you can run Java applets when you view Web pages that contain applets (see Chapter Five for more about Java applets). A browser named Opera, on the other hand, contains no built-in JVM, so you must add it yourself.

> ☆**WARNING** Internet Explorer and Java
>
> Just before this book went to press, Microsoft announced that it would no longer bundle the newest JVM in future releases of Internet Explorer. If you're an Internet Explorer user and you want to view Java applets that depend on the current JVM, you can make sure your browser is up to speed by installing a Java plug-in. For more information, see `http://java.sun.com/products/plugin/1.3/docs/quick_start.html`.

Just as you can customize your computer to reflect your needs and computing activities, you can also customize your browser to reflect your Web browsing needs and activities. When you customize your Web browser, you tell it how you want it to handle various types of files found on the Web. If you never want to hear WAV audio files, for example, you won't care if your browser can't handle them. But if WAV files are important to you, you may want your browser to use a specific player application whenever it encounters a WAV file on a Web page. If you want to view the Web with software you prefer, you can configure your browser to use the applications of your choice. Browsers can be configured to work with additional software through the use of plug-ins, add-ons, and helper applications.

Using Browser Plug-Ins

Plug-ins are applications that enhance your browser's viewing capabilities. When your browser encounters a file that requires a plug-in, the browser looks for an appropriate plug-in on your computer, launches it, and then loads the file. If you didn't have any plug-ins, you would have to download any special file found on the Web, save it to your hard drive, launch an appropriate application yourself, and open the downloaded file using that application. When you configure your browser to use a plug-in application, you're simply telling your browser to do all that for you automatically. When you configure your browser to use a plug-in, any file that requires the plug-in will be displayed inside the browser window.

Figure 3.1 shows Internet Explorer displaying a Word file with a Microsoft Word plug-in. Look at the drop-down menus on the right side of the second toolbar. Those are Word menus, not Internet Explorer menus. In other words, the plug-in doesn't simply give you a file display; it gives you the full functionality of the plugged-in application. Browser plug-ins are usually easy to set up because the download and installation processes are fully **scripted** (automated) for you.

Plug-Ins, Add-Ons, and Helper Applications

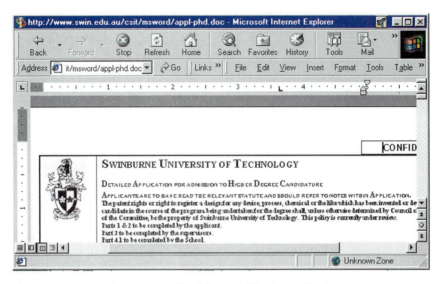

Figure 3.1 Internet Explorer Can Run Microsoft Word as a Plug-In

Adobe's Acrobat Reader is another example of a plug-in. If you rarely run into PDF files on the Web, you can always save them to disk and launch Acrobat as a separate application to view them (see Using Helper Applications to find out how to get your browser to launch an independent application). But if you regularly encounter PDF files, you should add Acrobat to your browser as a plug-in application.

The following list shows some popular plug-ins that you may find useful.

⭐ Adobe Acrobat Reader: Lets you view, navigate, and print PDF files

⭐ QuickTime: Displays QuickTime files as well as other video and audio file formats

⭐ PowerPoint Viewer, Excel Viewer, Word Viewer: Let you view and print Microsoft Office documents without installing these Office suite applications

⭐ RealPlayer: Plays various audio and video formats, including AU files (widely used for streaming audio)

⭐ Shockwave: Displays animation and documents produced with Macromedia Director or Flash

⭐ Windows Media Player: Displays popular streaming and local audio and video formats, including ASF, WAV, AVI, MPEG, QuickTime, and more

You can add plug-ins to your browser as you need them. If your browser tells you it doesn't know how to handle a particular file, that's when you can decide whether you want to add a plug-in.

Plug-Ins, Add-Ons, and Helper Applications

⭐ **SHORTCUT**   Netscape Navigator makes it easy to locate appropriate plug-ins on demand with its Plug-in Finder feature. As soon as you encounter a Web page that requires a plug-in, the Plug-in Finder figures out which one you need and offers it to you on the spot. To see which plug-ins have been added to Netscape Navigator, you can check the About Plug-ins feature (see Figure 3.2).

Figure 3.2 Check Your Personal Plug-in Library

Where Can I Find Plug-Ins for My Browser?

Both Netscape Navigator and Internet Explorer help you out with plug-in options whenever you visit a Web page that needs one. But if you want to browse the possibilities, here are some useful plug-in directories.

⭐ Official Netscape Plug-in Directory:
`http://home.netscape.com/plugins/index.html`

⭐ Plug-in Plaza:
`http://browserwatch.internet.com/plug-in.html`

⭐ ZDNet > Help & How-To > Internet > Plug-Ins:
`http://www.zdnet.com/zdhelp/filters/subfilter/`
`0,7212,6003243,00.html`

Using Browser Add-Ons

A **browser add-on** is an application that can be called from your browser either manually or automatically. To start an add-on manually, you click on a toolbar icon. The Alexa search facility is an example of an add-on (see Figure 3.3). Netscape distributes this add-on with Navigator (versions 4.06 and later) as part of its Smart Browsing services, and you can also download installers for Internet Explorer (versions 4.0 and later). To activate the Alexa add-on, you click the What's Related icon on the toolbar.

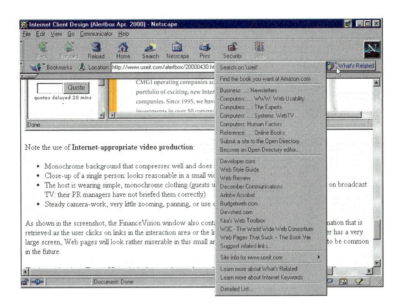

Figure 3.3 Navigator Users Launch Alexa from a Toolbar

To install an add-on, you download and install it just like any other software application. Most browser add-ons have their own executable installers (see Chapter Two). Figure 3.4 shows how you can integrate a meta search engine named Copernic with Internet Explorer as an add-on.

Figure 3.4 Integration Options in the Copernic Add-On

Sometimes an Internet application will be available as an add-on for some, but not all, browsers. For example, Copernic can be installed as an add-on for Internet Explorer but not for Netscape Navigator. If you install it as an add-on for Internet

Explorer, Internet Explorer creates a little toolbar icon for launching Copernic. If you aren't using Internet Explorer, you must launch Copernic from the Start menu or a desktop shortcut, just like any other application. You can still use Copernic with Netscape Navigator. If Netscape Navigator is your default browser, Copernic launches Navigator when you click on a hit in a Copernic hit list.

Using Helper Applications

A **helper application** can be any stand-alone application on your computer. Helper applications have been around longer than plug-ins and add-ons—and they do not integrate with browsers as easily as the other two. When your browser needs a helper application to open a file, it simply launches the application and asks it to open the file.

Here's how it works. When a browser encounters a file type it doesn't recognize, it suggests installing an appropriate plug-in (if one is available), or it asks the user what to do. Figure 3.5 shows the Opera Web browser asking the user what to do with a `.doc` (Word) file that it found inside a hyperlink. If the user has an application that can display a Word file, she can tell Opera where to find it. After Opera knows where to find an application suitable for `.doc` files, it will launch that application whenever it encounters a `.doc` file on the Web.

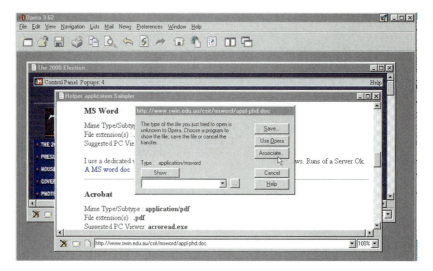

Figure 3.5 The Opera Web Browser Asks for Help with a .doc File

Figure 3.6 shows how Opera launches MS Word Viewer in a new window in order to display the `.doc` file. If you have MS Word Viewer, you can view Word files even if you don't have Word.

⭐ **SHORTCUT**   Word Viewer is a stripped-down version of Word. You can't use it to create or alter `.doc` files, but it does display them—and it's freeware.

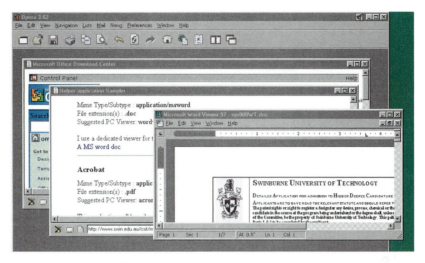

Figure 3.6 The Opera Web Browser Launches Word Viewer to Display a .doc File

◎◎ Download Managers

Large downloads don't always make it to your host machine in one piece. They fail for many reasons. For example, your host may crash during the download or get disconnected from the Internet before the download is completed. The server that is sending the file may crash, get disconnected, or experience bandwidth bottlenecks due to high traffic demands. A problem with an Internet gateway along the way can cause a disruption.

Browsers are prepared to download files, but they can complete the job only if there are no interruptions, no lost Internet connections, and no difficulties on the server's side. In addition, a large download over a slow telephone line can take an hour or two. This is a task you don't want to repeat. If you've ever had trouble downloading a file with your Web browser or if you download a lot of software or MP3 files, you'll appreciate the convenience of a good download manager.

If you're downloading a file and trouble strikes, you don't have many choices—you can restart the download from scratch, or you can give up. But a download manager can offer you other options. In most cases, the server will let you resume your original download where you left off. This is just what you want when the download is 98 percent complete and your telephone connection is dropped.

Let's look at some of the options available on a full-featured download manager: Go!Zilla for Windows (there are many comparable programs in this category). Figure 3.7 shows Go!Zilla in the middle of a large 2MB download.

Figure 3.7 Go!Zilla During a File Download

As you can see in the top window, the file is coming across at a rate of 3.3K per second, and the download can be resumed in case it gets interrupted. Not all servers can resume an interrupted download, so it's always best to work with a site that can. The download is 39 percent complete and is expected to take another five minutes. You can also see the location and name of the file being downloaded, and the location where it is being placed on the local host. You can see that the current server connection was established on the first try and that Go!Zilla was prepared to keep trying 100 times to make the connection. Apart from a few nice graphical effects (a colorful bandwidth chart as well as an artistic progress bar) and the convenience of being able to see where the file will be stored, the display doesn't look very different from your Web browser's progress bar. But there is more.

To the right of the bandwidth chart in the upper right-hand corner is a small speed control slider. When the slider is pushed all the way up, Go!Zilla is working at maximum speed. This is fine if you're not trying to do anything else with your computer during the download and you want the process to finish as quickly as possible. But if you're trying to surf the Web or run other programs while your download shuffles along in the background, you can adjust the speed control for a slower download.

If you unexpectedly need to reclaim your CPU or bandwidth, you can put the download on hold by pressing the Pause button. Because this download can be resumed, you can interrupt it and complete it later. Note that you can resume a partial download at any time, even if you need to disconnect from the Net and shut down your computer in the interim.

A good download manager starts working for you even before the download starts. In Figure 3.8 you see Go!Zilla's main download control window.

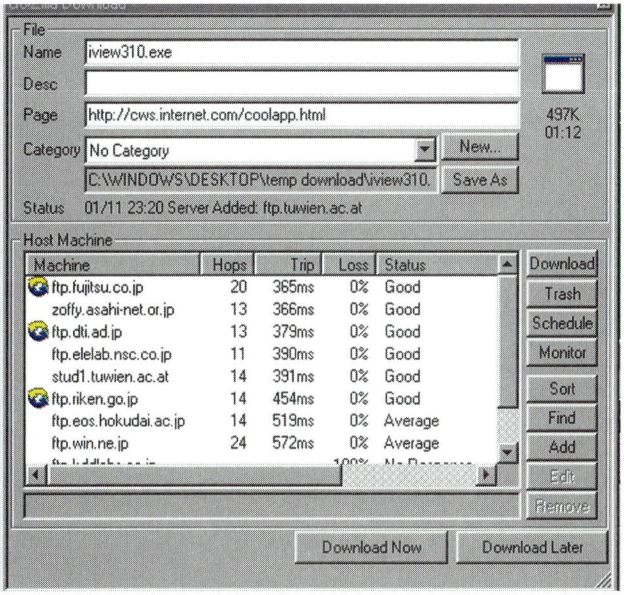

Figure 3.8 Go!Zilla Before a File Download

After you ask Go!Zilla to download a file, Go!Zilla uses specialized search engines to locate copies of the same file on other Web pages and File Transfer Protocol (FTP) servers. In this example, we're trying to download IrfanView (see Chapter Four), and we see that it's available on a number of servers, many of them in Japan. After Go!Zilla locates the candidate servers, it tests each one (see the Trip column) to find out how quickly that server responds. Go!Zilla then rates each server based on projected download times. You can see the Domain Name Server (DNS) address for each server as well as the number of intermediate hosts needed to get from here to there.

When you've seen enough, you can try to minimize your download time by picking a site with an excellent rating and a small number of hops. Or if none of the servers looks promising, you can schedule the download at a later time. Figure 3.9 shows how easy it is to pick a time and a day if you want to reschedule the download.

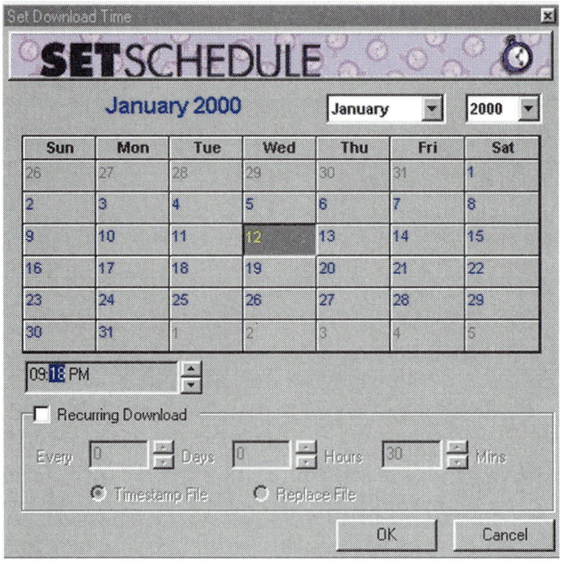

Figure 3.9 Go!Zilla's Download Scheduler

Because Go!Zilla can usually find the same file available on multiple servers, you can start a download on one server and then resume it on a different server. If you're having bad luck with the available servers, you may have to switch around to complete the download. In fact, Go!Zilla has a minimum transfer rate setting that it uses to optimize downloads even after they've been started. If the current transfer is not proceeding at the minimum transfer rate, Go!Zilla tries to speed up the remaining transfer by switching to the next best available server.

The following are some popular download managers:

⭐ Go!zilla Free (for Windows) (freeware):
   `http://www.gozilla.com/`

⭐ GetRight (for Windows) (shareware):
   `http://www.getright.com/`

⭐ Download Deputy (for Macintosh) (shareware):
   `http://www.ilesa.com/`

Some download managers are designed specifically for MP3s. Some of these search FTP servers, whereas others rely on a **peer-to-peer** model for file sharing. In peer-to-peer file sharing, users access the directories of other users rather than a large directory on a centralized server (Napster pioneered peer-to-peer MP3 sharing).

Most download managers are available as browser add-ons so that they're automatically invoked whenever you click on a download link. A good manager has many preference settings so that you can specify which file extensions should trigger the manager, where on your hard drive your download files should be saved, and whether you want to temporarily disable the download manager for any reason.

◉◉ Password Managers

Some of the best sites on the Web are available to registered users only. There's the news from The *New York Times* Online (`http://www.nytimes.com`), computer help forums for members at ZDNet (`http://www.zdnet.com/`), music downloads (`http://www.mp3.com`), and countless Web-based mail services.

If you like to visit sites like these, you have a problem. If you give each site a unique identifier and password, it's difficult to remember which IDs and which passwords go with which sites. Using the same keywords at each site is easier, but it jeopardizes your online security. If your login information should be compromised at one site, it will be compromised at all your other sites. Commercial sites that have collected your credit card information will release that information to anyone who can successfully enter your registration ID and password. Sites that have collected sensitive personal information (such as health-related sites) will release that information to anyone who logs in as you. To be as safe as possible, you should use different IDs and passwords at each site that requires a login, even if you're dealing with dozens of password-protected sites. This is where password managers pay off.

A **password manager** is a small program that keeps track of login information for you. It's like an address book except that it holds information needed to visit protected Web sites. You may have tried to create your own password manager by simply keeping notes in a text file. This solution is better than nothing if it encourages you to use unique identifiers at each site. But if that file is compromised by a security lapse on your local host, you're in trouble again.

These kinds of complications may have discouraged you from registering at many Web sites. Avoiding these sites is a solution of sorts, but you're depriving yourself of some good online resources.

A good password manager is the best solution. Figure 3.10 shows a Web site entry from a freeware password manager named Password Prompter (`http://www.zdnet.com/pcmag/pctech/content/18/11/ut1811.001.html`).

Each time you register at a Web site, you create a new directory entry for that site. When you later return to that site, you look it up in Password Prompter's site directory and transfer the password using a copy-and-paste command.

Note that the asterisks in Figure 3.10 only mask the actual password characters in the directory display. If you copy and paste these asterisks into a text editor, the actual password will be visible. A good password manager protects its information with encryption and its own password-protection on startup (see Figure 3.11).

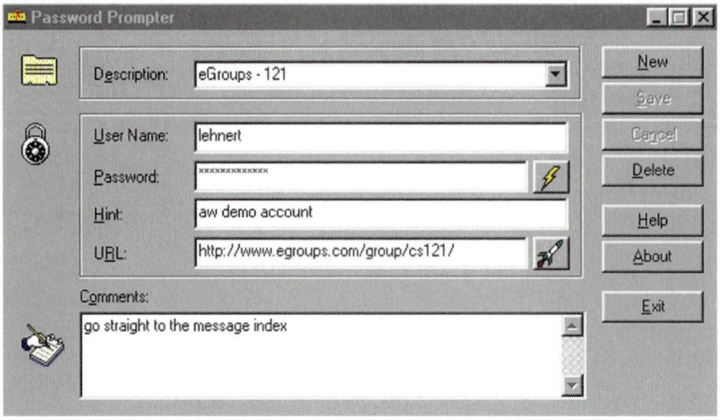

Figure 3.10 Password Prompter Organizes and Protects Sensitive Ids

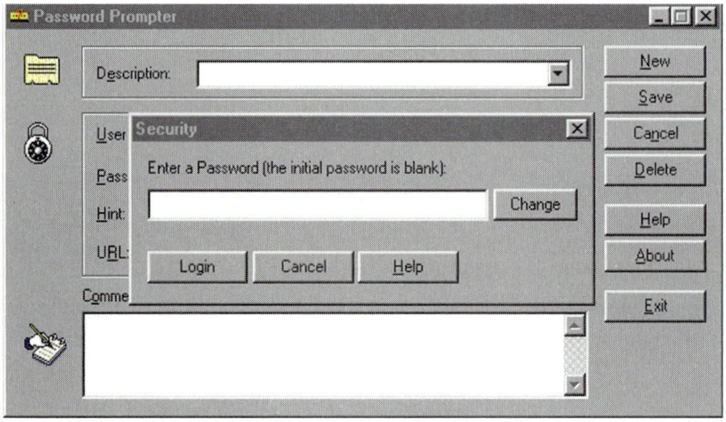

Figure 3.11 You Only Need to Remember One Password

A useful feature is a randomizing password generator. When you register at a site for the first time, you ask your password manager for a randomized password instead of making one up yourself (see Figure 3.12). Randomized passwords are more secure than human-generated passwords because they do not contain any recognizable words or name substrings. You aren't trying to remember any of these passwords yourself, so you don't need a password that's easy to remember. A random password is much better.

It's easy to find applications such as Password Prompter (use the query "password manager" at a software clearinghouse), and they'll save you from ever forgetting a password again. Just be careful not to forget the master password! But you do have to launch them each time you need a password, and you must manually retrieve the desired password. If this proves to be too annoying, look for a password manager that can be integrated into your browser as a browser add-on.

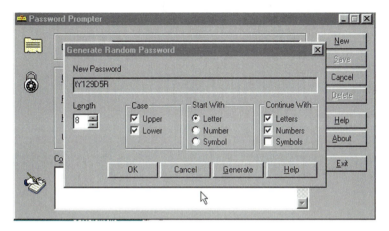

Figure 3.12 A Randomized Password Generator

⭐ **WARNING** **Protect Your Credit Card Number**

If you do a lot of online shopping, it's convenient to have your credit card information written in a file for easy lookup. But if you do, you're taking a risk each time you connect to the Internet (this risk is greater if you have a broadband connection). You can eliminate all such risk by storing such sensitive information in a password directory utility. For example, Password Prompter gives you a comment field for each entry, so you can create any entry you want. Everything you store in these comment fields will be encrypted for safety against prying eyes (including snoopy roommates or officemates, inquisitive hackers, or your own curious children). Only you will be able to retrieve it using your master password.

Gator (http://www.gator.com/) is an example of a utility that not only handles Web site passwords but also operates as an assistant for Web page forms in general. It records site IDs, passwords, and other frequently required information each time you visit a Web page that requests them. At subsequent visits to one of those pages, Gator pops up and offers to fill in the form. Instead of typing lots of routine information, you just click one Gator button and you're finished. You can control which sites Gator responds to (see Figure 3.13), and you can change Gator's entries for any site at any time. Gator is password-protected, and all its data is encrypted for maximum security, as with Password Prompter. To find programs such as Gator, use the query "form fill" at a software clearinghouse.

In sum, passwords are an important component in maintaining secure systems, and you should do everything you can to keep your passwords secure. Whatever you do, avoid using the same password in a dozen different places. It's easier to remember only one password, but with the right software in place, you can maintain separate passwords for all your Web registrations without having to remember more than one password. Remember, it's always easier to prevent a security problem than it is to fix one.

Password Managers

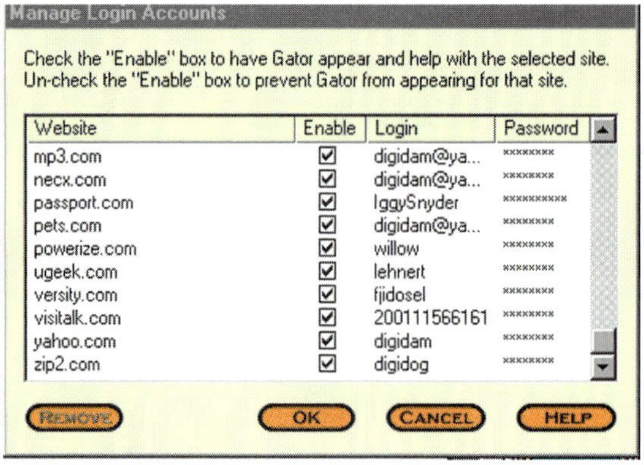

Figure 3.13 A Customized Site Directory in Gator

◎◎ Cookie Managers and Ad Filters

One of the most controversial data collection practices on the Web involves the use of cookies. A **cookie** is a file created by a Web server and stored on your host machine by your Web browser. It's a small file that patiently awaits your next visit to the Web. Any Web server can check to see whether you have a cookie file and, if so, whether it has any useful information about you. For example, suppose that the last time you visited a particular site, you spent all your time at two particular pages. A cookie can record this information, and the next time you visit the site, the server might greet you with a page display that makes it especially easy to navigate to those pages.

Cookies allow Web servers to create a profile about you and your activities. Parts of this profile may have been collected with your assistance (for example, you must tell it your name if you want a personal greeting). Other parts may be deduced from your past interactions with the server.

Cookie files can be used to make life easier for a Web user. Amazon.com, for example, tracks the books you browse when you visit its pages so that the company can offer recommendations next time you visit its site. The more time you spend looking at books, the better these recommendations are likely to be. *The New York Times* on the Web is free but requires visitors to register with a name and a password. Then a cookie can be installed that checks for your name and password each time you return. This means that you can enter the site automatically without having to enter your name or password, as though the site were unrestricted. This is particularly convenient for people who have a lot of passwords and have trouble remembering them.

Cookies are also used to target potential customers with banner ads. For example, if you visit the Netly News at `pathfinder.com`, the site records any of your mouse clicks that reveal an interest in specific technologies. A resulting cookie may be used the next time you visit Pathfinder to show you an ad about a product that reflects your apparent interests. For more details about how cookies and banner ads are used to create consumer profiles, visit `Privacy.net`.

On the one hand, you might feel that cookies provide a useful service. Maybe you would like to hear about products and promotions that might be of interest to you. On the other hand, you might also want to be reassured that all this information about your reading habits, consumer spending, recreational activities, and so on is not being sold to information brokers and marketing companies. At the very least, you might want to be informed if a Web site is going to put a cookie on your hard drive.

In an effort to respect your privacy, most Web browsers now ask users for permission to install a cookie (for example, the most recent versions of Navigator and Internet Explorer are "cookie-correct"). Figure 3.14 shows a **cookie alert** box that appears when a Web server asks a Web client for permission to create a cookie.

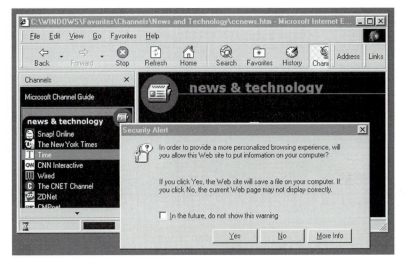

Figure 3.14 Your Browser Can Ask You Permission for a Cookie

This query is asking for permission to create a cookie file or add an entry to your existing cookie file. You can accept or reject the request, and your browser will proceed as instructed. You can also instruct your browser not to bother you with any more cookie requests during this visit to this host (some Web sites create multiple cookies for each user). Each time you restart your browser and return to the site in a new browser session, you'll have to respond to an initial cookie query again, but at least you can avoid some of the cookie requests.

You can also opt to avoid all cookie requests by reconfiguring your browser's preference settings. Figure 3.15 shows the options available to Internet Explorer users. You can opt to accept all cookies unconditionally, reject all cookies unconditionally, or be prompted with cookie alerts to review all cookie requests. Figure 3.16 shows a Web page that asks users if they would like the Web page to remember their password. When a user opts for this feature, the password is stored in a cookie.

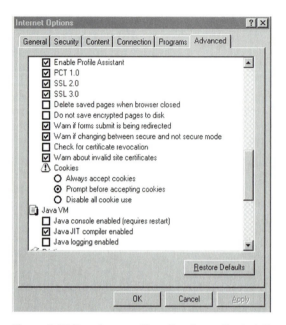

Figure 3.15 Your Browser Gives You Some Control Over Cookies

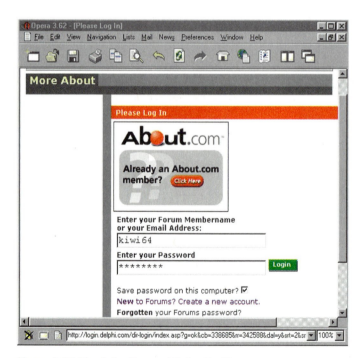

Figure 3.16 Check the Box and Get a Cookie

The pros and cons of cookies are a hotly debated topic among Netizens. Most people are more comfortable with cookies when they can exercise some control over who is allowed to create them. Exercising this control takes time, however, so some people prefer to automatically block all cookie requests in order to maintain maximum privacy and streamline their Web sessions. If you want more power over which cookies you accept and reject and you don't want to be bothered with cookie alerts, software is available for managing cookies.

> ⭐ **TIP   An Enhanced Cookie Manager**
>
> Much like the most popular cookie managers, Netscape Navigator 6 supports site-specific and cookie-specific management options. At the time of this writing, Internet Explorer's cookie management options are still limited, but Microsoft may incorporate cookie management controls based on new P3P privacy standards in future versions of Internet Explorer.

> ⭐ **TIP   Cookies Can Be Useful**
>
> Cookies make the following things possible:
> - ★ Online shopping carts for e-commerce sites
> - ★ Automatic logins to restricted sites (such as Web-based discussion groups and e-mail accounts)
> - ★ Personalized Web portals that show you only the things you care about
>
> If you disable all cookies, you won't be able to use these features.

Privacy, Spam, and User Profiling

The controversy over cookies is based on concerns about user profiling, consumer consent, and privacy violations. Each cookie can be read only by servers from the domain of the Web site responsible for the cookie. A cookie created by one Web server at yahoo.com, for example, can be read only by other servers at yahoo.com.

It would be reassuring to know that personal information stays within the confines of the site that collected it and is not being sold to marketers and third-party vendors. Privacy policies at many commercial Web sites have begun to address consumer concerns. Responsible e-commerce sites post **notice-and-consent** check boxes, where visitors can opt out of data resale operations. But these policies protect only the data collected by the in-house Web servers, and most commercial data collection is done by ad servers (discussed next). Few consumers understand how ad servers operate, let alone how to track them down in order to opt out of their notice-and-consent option (if they even have one). Ad servers and their privacy policies worry privacy advocates, especially because the general public is largely unaware of the fact that banner ads can collect data about you even if you never click on them.

An **ad server** is a special-purpose Web server that feeds ads to Web sites. A banner ad on a commercial Web page is often housed on an independent ad server rather than a server at the parent site. DoubleClick, the leading ad server, delivers more than one billion ads per day. Other ad servers are responsible for another one or two billion ads per week. These numbers will only grow as time goes on.

When you visit a page at yahoo.com, you may view a banner ad from a third-party ad server such as DoubleClick. Banner ads from ad servers are often paired with cookies. If you accept a cookie from an ad server, it can be accessed and read by the server whenever new material (such as another banner ad) is downloaded from that ad server or any other server in the same domain. None of this is explained to the user, and few people take the time to learn about cookies and how they are used by ad servers.

Proponents of user profiling often argue that no identifying information is associated with the data collected by cookies: The cookie ID numbers that make it possible to collect user profiles do not reveal user names, addresses, or other information. However, sensitive identifiers can be captured by Web forms and passed along to third-party data brokers, with or without cookies.

You may therefore conclude that you can protect your identity by (1) not telling your browser your name or e-mail address and (2) checking the privacy policies for any site that requests identifying information. As long as you withhold information from all sites that do not promise to keep that information confidential, you should be safe, right? Unfortunately, the answer is no.

If you read your e-mail with an HTML-enhanced e-mail client, chances are that your largest user profiles have already been connected to your e-mail address. And if data brokers have your e-mail address, they probably have your name and address as well (have you ever filled out a form for a store that asks for your e-mail address?).

Here's how it works. It starts when you open a piece of mail from a mail spammer (see Figure 3.17). If the message contains a 1×1-pixel GIF image located on an ad server, you've just handed your e-mail address over to the ad server. Let's suppose the spammer is an outfit named Spam-O-Rama and the company that runs the ad server is named Tracker. Before Spam-O-Rama sends one of its mailings to 30 million e-mail addresses, it sells one pixel of space in its message body to Tracker. This means that Tracker can insert a URL to its ad server in the mail message. Tracker inserts an invisible GIF located on its ad server, so one pixel is all the space Tracker needs.

Each time this message goes out from Spam-O-Rama, the URL for Tracker's GIF can be modified to include the e-mail address of the current recipient, much as URLs can be modified to include keywords from search engine queries. Then when the recipient opens this message with an HTML-enabled e-mail client, the GIF file is downloaded and the recipient's e-mail address is sent back to Tracker's ad server.

When the URL request arrives at Tracker's ad server, the ad server extracts the address from the URL and launches a script to collect more information from the recipient's Web browser (the recipient's HTML-enabled e-mail client is running a Web browser to read this mail). The script asks the browser for any cookies from Tracker's domain, and if the browser can find any, they are sent to Tracker. If a cookie is found, its ID number is connected to the recently obtained e-mail address, and if a user profile is available for that ID number, the e-mail address can now be added to that profile (see Figure 3.17).

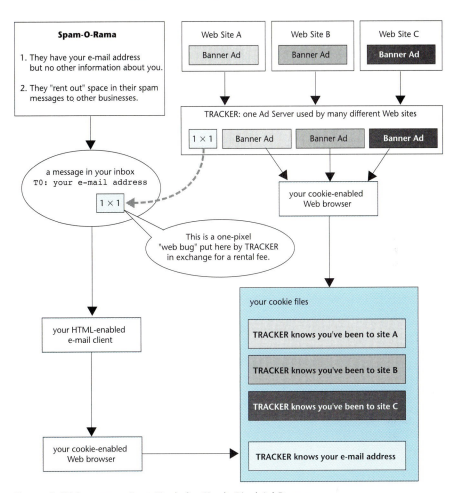

Figure 3.17 Spammers Rent Pixels for Single-Pixel Ad Banners

One-pixel banner ads are sometimes called **Web bugs**. They don't threaten your system security, but they are a blatant violation of personal privacy. You can foil the Web bugs by (1) never reading anything that looks like spam, (2) setting up ad filters for all the biggest ad server operations, (3) setting up cookie filters for the biggest ad server operations, or (4) turning off the graphics for your browser when you read your e-mail. If that one-pixel GIF image is never downloaded from the ad server, it cannot send your e-mail address back to the server.

As mentioned earlier, some cookies are useful (especially if you want to do any online shopping), but others are nothing but a threat to your privacy. Unfortunately, Web browsers do not offer an adequate strategy for managing cookies. If you set your browser preferences to reject all cookies, you won't be able to use shopping carts at e-stores. If you set your browser to accept all cookies, ad servers will compile a user profile on you. If you tell your browser to ask you what to do with each cookie that is offered, you'll go crazy with all the pop-up windows.

But don't despair—there is a solution. Read on.

Cookie Managers

Happily, there is a solution to the problem of cookies. All you need is a **cookie manager**, a utility that lets you apply a default policy for cookies in general while specifying different policies for specific Web sites. In that way, you can create a default rejection policy to protect you from the ad servers and customized policies for your favorite e-stores and member-only discussion groups (see Figure 3.18).

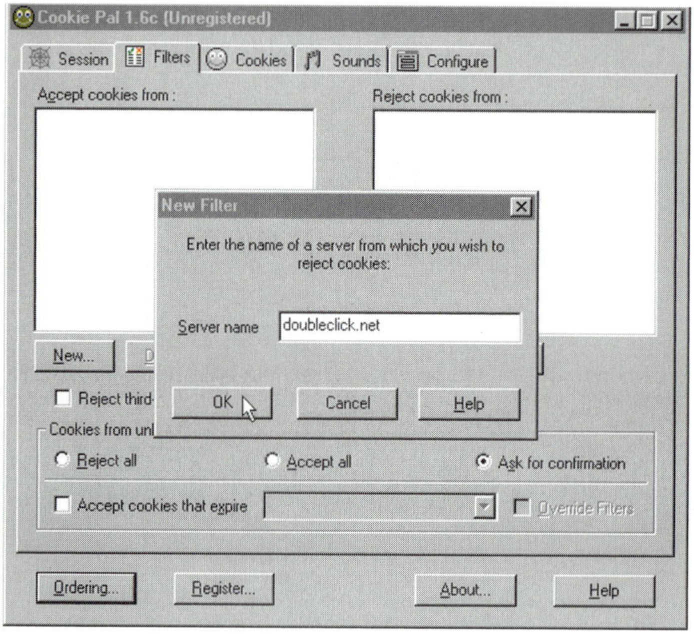

Figure 3.18 The Cookie Pal Cookie Manager

Cookie managers can also show you a world of Web activity that is normally hidden from your view. Most cookie managers collect a log of their activities for you to review. Figure 3.19 shows a log generated by AdSubtract after a single browsing session. AdSubtract can filter both ads and cookies, and that makes it easy to see the ad servers. Notice how DoubleClick generated a cookie for each ad, and herring.com generated more cookies than ads.

Many cookie managers are available on the Net. The freeware options are more limited than their shareware counterparts, but they all give you more control than you get from your Web browser's preference settings. Some cookie managers can block ads as well as cookies, minimizing the amount of work needed to set up all the different filters.

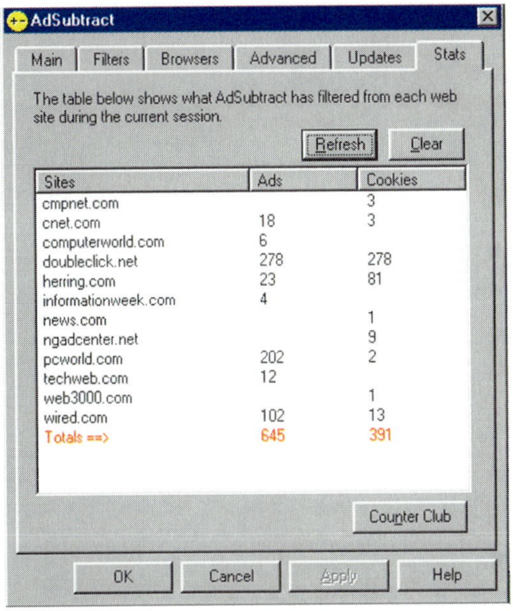

Figure 3.19 A Look Behind the Scenes during a Browsing Session

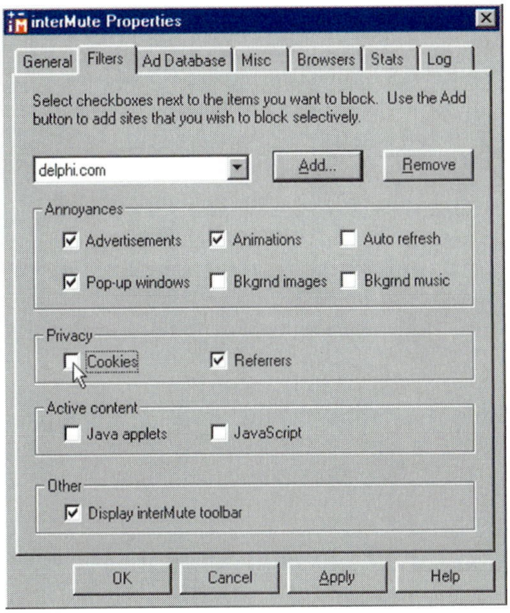

Figure 3.20 The AdSubtract (interMute, Inc.) Cookie Manager

The best cookie managers do not ask you to set a policy for each site that you visit, something that becomes tedious if you visit a lot of different Web sites. It's much easier to set up a default policy that's applied to all sites unless you choose to create a special filter for a specific site. This eases the task of creating a customized plan for cookie management.

Dealing with cookies may seem like an inconvenience and an annoyance, but the right software makes everything painless. Don't settle for the first cookie manager you find. They're not all the same, and the first one you try might not be the best one for you. Research the most popular cookie managers, read the reviews, and test-drive one or two managers before you make your decision. When you get your cookies under control, they'll never bother you again.

> ☆**TIP**   **Some Popular Cookie Managers:**
>
> ★ CookiePal (shareware for Windows): `http://www.kburra.com/`
> ★ Cookie Crusher (shareware for Windows): `http://www.thelimitsoft.com/`
> ★ AdSubtract SE (freeware for Windows): `http://adsubtract.com/`
> ★ MagicCookie Monster (freeware for the Mac): `http://download.at/drjsoftware`

Ad Filters

Most people who talk about filters for Web browsers are usually talking about software that censors content to make the Web safe for children. But that's not what this section is about. Here, I'm talking about **ad filters**, which work to remove ad banners and other advertisements from your Web page displays. Some ad filters can be configured to remove ads, freeze animated GIFs, and censor objectionable images (as specified by the user). Some people use ad filters because they get tired of seeing advertisements all the time. Others use them to speed up their Web page displays.

On most Web pages, an ad filter can be counted on to find and remove banner ads (see Figure 3.21).

One of the most popular ad filters is WebWasher, which is distributed by Siemens Corporation as freeware for home and educational use. WebWasher identifies and removes banner ads, pop-up ads, and animated graphics. Anyone can install WebWasher on a personal computer to filter out ads on Web pages. A network administrator can install WebWasher to filter out content for everyone on a company's local area network. Many corporations "wash" Web pages to keep employees more focused and less distracted. One could argue that this is a form of censorship, but private companies can censor anything they want within the confines of the workplace. WebWasher has been shown to reduce bandwidth consumption within a workplace network by as much as 45 percent.

Are Banner Ads Really So Terrible?

You may not think that ads on the Internet are all that bad. After all, we live with ads on television and radio, ads in newspapers and magazines, and ads on billboards, buses, telephone poles, and sports venues. Why should the Internet be any different?

Figure 3.21 A Web Page With and Without Ad Filtering

Well, the Internet *is* different. For one thing, the cost of Internet advertising is minimal and doesn't reflect the shared resources consumed and the cost to everyone who uses the Internet. For example, each ad posted on a Web page and downloaded by a Web browser consumes bandwidth, and bandwidth is a limited resource. If too many ads are consuming too much bandwidth, download times increase for everyone, and Internet usage patterns can be affected. For example, visit `ZDNet.com` over a phone line and try to browse the site. Chances are, you'll find yourself waiting a long time for the pages to download. During a recent visit to ZDNet with a 56K modem, one ad filter trapped roughly 60 ads per minute. As a result, it's nearly impossible to browse this site without a broadband connection.

Companies who advertise on the Web tend to view their ad banners and pop-up windows as an essential part of the e-commerce business model. As a result, commercial advertisers are not pleased with the idea of content filters. The widespread adaptation of ad filtering technology would strike at the heart of their enterprises and threaten their ability to recover advertising costs. And if the advertisers fall, Web sites subsidized by advertisers presumably will follow, and the commercialization of the Web could be dealt a serious blow. But that's a hypothetical scenario, and it's far from inevitable. Even the advertisers realize that technical options such as content filters are better for them than government regulations or laws designed to restrict commercial advertising on the Web.

Although advertisers can only speculate about their future on the Web, network administrators must deal with the effects of too many ad banners and pop-up windows right now. Network administrators are forced to absorb the financial costs of unwanted advertisements on their networks. These ads, which are disseminated over the Internet at no cost to the advertisers, consume bandwidth and impair the performance of the Internet for everyone (businesspeople, researchers, educators, and students). Consumers should have a right to opt out of the advertising stream, and commercial advertisers should not assume that it is their right to profit from resources that they do not pay for.

> ★ **TIP   Some Popular Ad Filtering Software**
>
> ★ WebWasher (freeware for PCs): `http://www.siemens.de/servers/wwash/wwash_us.htm`
> ★ Internet Junkbusters (freeware for PCs): `http://www.junkbusters.com/`
> ★ AdSubtract SE (freeware for PCs): `http://www.adsubtract.com/`
> ★ AdSubtract Pro (shareware for PCs): `http://www.adsubtract.com/se/upgrade.html`
> ★ WebFree (shareware for Macintosh): `http://www.falken.net/webfree/`
>
> Some cookie managers also offer excellent ad filtering capabilities.

User Profiling and Banner Ads

Some ad servers collect personal data from browsers that merely display banner ads. The user does not have to click on the ad or do anything else except download the Web page containing the banner ad.

Here's how it works. Each time a Web page containing the ad is generated, adjustments are made to the URL for the banner ad. For example, suppose you visit `lycos.com` and conduct a search using the keyword "prozac." When Lycos returns the list of hits for this query, you'll see a URL for a DoubleClick banner ad that includes the keyword "prozac."

The referring URL (this is the URL for the hit list returned by Lycos) is `http://www.lycos.com/srch/?lpv=1&loc=searchhp&query=`**`prozac`**`&x=31&y=8`

The banner ad URL (this is the URL for a banner ad that appears on the hit list page) is `http://ln.doubleclick.net/jump/ly.ln/r;kw=`**`prozac`**`;pos=1;sz=468x60;tile=1;ratio=1_2;! ... (etc.) ...`

These unusual-looking URLs do not simply return files from Web servers; rather, they execute special scripts (small executable programs) on their respective servers. The script triggered by the referring URL sends a search query to the Lycos search engine. Then when the search engine returns its hits, the script on the Lycos server creates a Web page designed to display those hits, and this hit list page also contains the URL for the DoubleClick banner ad. The banner ad URL triggers another script, but this one is on a DoubleClick server.

Among other things, this script returns the banner ad that you see on the page of search engine hits. You have no way of knowing for sure what else the DoubleClick script does, but you can see from the banner ad URL that the keyword "prozac" is given to the script. If DoubleClick has sold this particular keyword to one of its advertisers, that advertiser's banner ad will be delivered by the DoubleClick ad server. It would also be easy for the DoubleClick script to store this keyword in a database of Lycos search engine queries if DoubleClick wants to keep track of all the queries sent to the Lycos search engine.

Collecting keyword queries such as "prozac" is not a problem if that's all the script does. But if the user sending this query to Lycos has ever accepted a cookie from DoubleClick, then the DoubleClick server can associate this query with a unique DoubleClick ID number stored in the cookie—and that makes it possible for DoubleClick to group a number of queries under a common ID number. If the cookie is programmed to persist for years, a large number of keywords could be collected, saved, and associated with the same DoubleClick ID number.

Additionally, any other search engines that display banner ads from DoubleClick can also send their query keywords to the same DoubleClick script. Then those queries will be associated with the same unique DoubleClick ID number (see Figure 3.22).

In the same way, DoubleClick can amass personal information from Web pages that collect names, addresses, e-mail addresses, and other personal information that users type into forms, and all this information would be grouped under the same unique ID number. If you visit enough Web sites that display banner ads from DoubleClick, DoubleClick can accumulate a lot of valuable information about you and your interests.

A collection of data about a single user is called a **user profile**. DoubleClick says that extensive user profiles are good for users because accurate user profiles make it possible for DoubleClick to send banner ads that better target the needs and interests of individual users. Privacy advocates, on the other hand, are worried about user profiles being sold to third parties and consolidated with other database profiles in an effort to build even larger profiles. Moreover, any identifying information that makes its way into these profiles can be used to associate the profile with more than a cookie's ID number. A user profile that can be connected to a person or even just an e-mail address is a valuable commodity.

If you take a look at online instructions for setting up a content filter on your home computer, you get the impression that these things are more trouble than they're worth. For example, the Junkbuster filter's FAQ (frequently asked questions) page has a tendency to scare people because it is so thorough; it does an excellent job of covering all the possible trouble spots. In truth, some filters are easier to set up than others. The Junkbuster filter can be fully customized, but this makes it more complicated than some of the simpler filters. Don't try Junkbusters unless you're patient and willing to spend some time on it. If you want to keep things simple, WebWasher is easy to set up, although you will still have to change some browser proxy settings yourself. If you're looking for the easiest installation, try AdSubtract SE. If you're working on a Macintosh, WebFree is both easy to customize and easy to install.

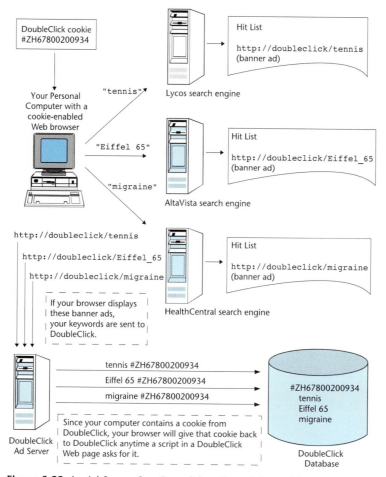

Figure 3.22 An Ad Server Can Consolidate Data Collected from a Single Host Machine

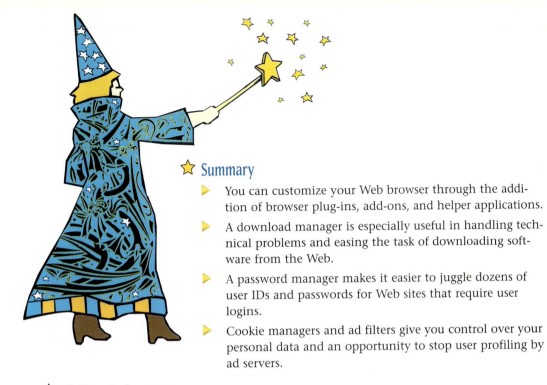

⭐ Summary

▶ You can customize your Web browser through the addition of browser plug-ins, add-ons, and helper applications.

▶ A download manager is especially useful in handling technical problems and easing the task of downloading software from the Web.

▶ A password manager makes it easier to juggle dozens of user IDs and passwords for Web sites that require user logins.

▶ Cookie managers and ad filters give you control over your personal data and an opportunity to stop user profiling by ad servers.

⭐ Online References

Help! Plug-Ins.
http://www1.sympatico.ca/help/Plugins/

Learn the Net: Plug-Ins.
http://www.learnthenet.com/english/html/56plugins.htm

Cookie Central
http://cookiecentral.com/

Junkbusters
http://www.junkbusters.com/

⭐ Review Questions

1. Explain the difference between a browser plug-in and a browser add-on.

2. Explain the difference between a browser plug-in and a helper application.

3. Each of the following is either a browser plug-in or a browser add-on. Which is which?
   (a) Copernic 2000 (a meta search engine that can be launched from Internet Explorer's toolbar)
   (b) Adobe Acrobat Reader (displays PDF files)
   (c) Shockwave (displays animation files by Macromedia Director)
   (d) QuickTime (displays various video and audio file formats)
   (e) Go!Zilla (a download manager that's launched when you click on a link to a file)

71

4. What is an ad server? How much traffic do ad servers produce?

5. How can you prevent someone from creating a detailed user profile of you based on your Web surfing behavior? Is it enough to turn off the graphics in your Web browser? Explain your answer.

6. Name four things that a download manager can do that a Web browser can't do.

7. How can you protect sensitive credit card information on your home computer? Name one software program that would be useful for this.

8. How is a download manager different from an FTP client? Does anyone need both? Explain your answer.

9. Explain two ways that password managers help you stay secure online.

10. What is a Web bug? Who plants them, and where are they found? Who benefits from Web bugs?

★ Hands-On Exercises

1. Select, download, and install a plug-in for your browser that you would like to try (pick one other than Adobe Acrobat Reader). Test it on a suitable page to make sure it works. Keep a log of your activities so that you can answer the following questions:

   (a) Which plug-in did you select?
   (b) Describe where you found the plug-in (give a URL).
   (c) How long did it take you to install it?
   (d) Did it work right away?
   (e) Provide a URL where this plug-in is used.

   Describe any difficulties that you experienced with this exercise.

2. Download and install the latest Adobe Acrobat Reader plug-in. How does your browser display change when you download a PDF file? (You will find lots of PDF files at http://www.planetpdf.com/).

3. If you use Netscape Navigator, pull down the Help menu and select About Plug-ins to find out how many plug-ins have been installed in your browser. How many are there? List them. Which of these did you install yourself (as opposed to the plug-ins that come with your browser)?

4. Select, download, and install a download manager that you would like to try. Make sure your download manager is integrated with your browser (when you click on a file link, your browser should automatically launch your download manager). Where does your download manager place files on your hard drive?

5. Select, download, and install a cookie manager or an ad filter. Can you find a log of all the cookies or ads that have been caught and rejected during a browser session? If so, check this log after a typical browsing session. Which site was responsible for the most cookies or ads?

CHAPTER FOUR

ESSENTIAL TOOLS FOR WEB PAGE AUTHORS

f you know the basics of HTML, you can create all your Web pages using nothing more than a simple text editor and a Web browser. A plain text editor is useful in a pinch, but it's far from ideal if you do a lot of Web page design. If you have a few hundred dollars you can invest in a comprehensive Web design tool kit such as Microsoft FrontPage or Macromedia Dreamweaver. But there are plenty of Web tools available online at little or no cost if you're willing to hunt a bit and collect your software piecemeal. With a little time and patience, you can probably find a freeware or shareware utility for everything you want to do.

Chapter Objectives

⭐ Find out what a freeware FTP client can do for you

⭐ Look at freeware HTML editors and HTML validators

⭐ See what you can do with freeware and shareware graphics utilities

★ Investigate freeware and shareware link checkers

★ Learn how to save time with image mappers

★ See what other special purpose utilities are available as freeware

◎◎ FTP Clients

The File Transfer Protocol (FTP) is one of the oldest Internet protocols, and **FTP clients** are the oldest file sharing programs on the Internet. If you need to move multiple files from one Internet host to another, an FTP client is the way to do it (Web pages can be uploaded to Web servers via FTP clients). All file types can be transferred, including all binary formats, and the speed of the transmission is limited only by the speed of your modem. If your local host is connected directly to the Internet via an Ethernet or cable modem connection, large FTP file transfers are completed in a matter of seconds.

Moreover, FTP is not limited to files on Web servers. People also find it useful for uploading files to shared directories when they collaborate on major projects. For example, each chapter of this book was uploaded to an FTP server so that everyone involved in its production could work with the files.

When you use an FTP client to visit an FTP server, you start by specifying the domain name or Internet Protocol (IP) address of the host machine you want to contact. If you don't know which FTP server to visit, your FTP client can't help you.

Figure 4.1 shows the opening window of a graphical FTP client named WS_FTP LE, a program available as freeware for noncommercial use. You type the domain name address of the target server in the Host Name/Address field. In this example, we're initiating an anonymous FTP connection, so we type "anonymous" in the User ID field and type a complete e-mail address as the password (this is set during installation). When all the required entries are complete, you click OK and WS_FTP LE looks for an FTP server at the specified host address.

★SHORTCUT Clicking the Anonymous check box fills in the user ID automatically.

Figure 4.2 shows WS_FTP LE in action after the FTP connection has been established. Two directories are displayed: one for the local host (on the left) and one for the remote FTP server (on the right). You can navigate the directory hierarchies using scrolling and point-and-click. To download a file, you select the file name on the remote server and click the arrow pointing to the left. The file will be copied to the current directory (shown in the window) on the local host. To upload a file, you select the file name on the local host and click the arrow pointing to the right. The file will be copied to the current directory (shown in the window) on the remote host.

Graphical FTP clients have many convenient features that make FTP fast and painless. For example, most FTP clients create a separate window for any welcome messages, so you can easily refer to them at any time. If you need to move a lot of files at once (such as an entire Web site), an FTP client will let you queue up entire subdirectories so that you don't have to move each file one by one. Some FTP clients also let you view files remotely on an FTP server without downloading them, and a few let you edit text files remotely if you are running a full-privilege FTP session (this requires a personal computer account on the remote host). Remote editing is handy when you maintain a Web site and need to make a few small corrections or updates to a page.

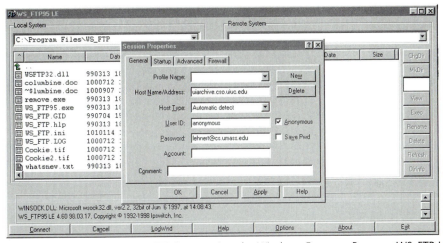

Figure 4.1 Connecting to an FTP Server using the Windows Freeware Program WS_FTP LE

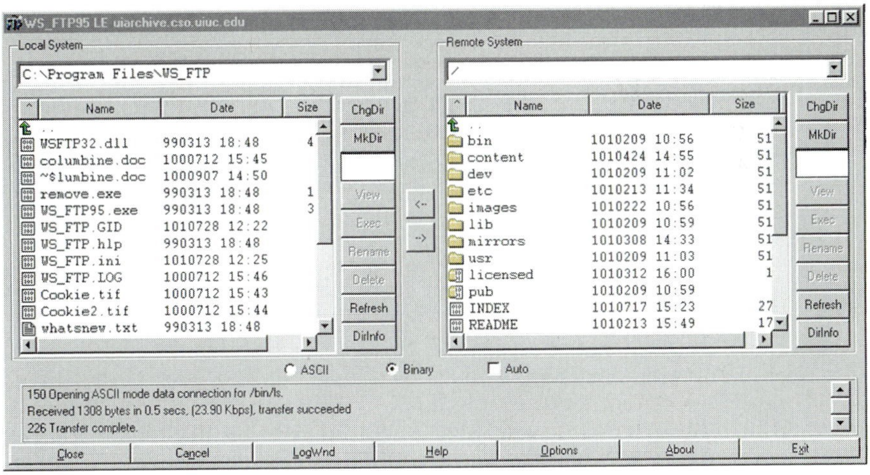

Figure 4.2 Viewing the Current Local and Remote Directories

There are many graphical FTP clients for Mac and PC platforms, and all of them are easy to use. A good FTP client has these useful features:

⭐ Simultaneous displays of local and remote directories

⭐ Sorting options for directory displays

⭐ Support for multiple FTP sessions running in parallel

★ Support for multiple file transfers

★ Resumable file transfers (in case a transfer is interrupted)

★ A timer (so that you can schedule large jobs during meetings or after bedtime)

★ Intuitive drag-and-drop file transfers

★ An address book for automated logins on different servers

★ File search facilities

FTP servers are often used when a group of colleagues need to share files. A project directory is created on a password-protected FTP server so that the files are available only to the project participants. They can then download and upload files to the FTP server via full-privilege FTP sessions. This is the easiest way to share files within a geographically dispersed workforce, especially when a large number of files are involved or when the files are very big.

E-mail attachments are sometimes used, but e-mail tends to be cumbersome when there are a great many files, people, or file updates. E-mail also assumes that the recipient is ready to receive and file a document whenever it arrives, something that can be intrusive and inconvenient for people who manage large amounts of e-mail. With an FTP server, both the sender and the recipient can choose to access the server at the most convenient time.

◎◎ HTML Editors and Validators

HTML editors are easy to use and wonderful time-savers. You can either buy a commercial package or take advantage of excellent freeware options, such as Arachnophilia. Pull-down menus and toolbars give you everything you need to point-and-click your way to a Web page.

Figure 4.3 shows how Arachnophilia gets you off the ground after you create a new HTML file and enter the title "The Dachshund." The basic HTML template is created automatically and is ready for you to add HTML elements. In Arachnophilia, a preview window displays your page in your browser, so you can watch the page develop as you go. Other packages, such as Netscape Communicator's Composer, give you a **WYSIWYG (what you see is what you get)** editor that lets you modify a displayed version of your page rather than the underlying HTML file. WYSIWYG editors try to distance Web page authors from the underlying HTML as much as possible to make design a no-brainer.

Even the simpler HTML editors watch what you type and color-code your tags, tag attributes, and tag attribute values as you type them. This gives you immediate feedback if you make a syntax error, clearly marking the location of the error. Arachnophilia is a good choice for people who are just getting started with HTML. It offers a solid selection of authoring tools in a friendly, intuitive interface.

For more experienced and advanced users, HTML-Kit, another freeware utility, offers a larger selection of authoring tools, including Cascading Style Sheet options and converters for XML and XHTML (see Figure 4.4).

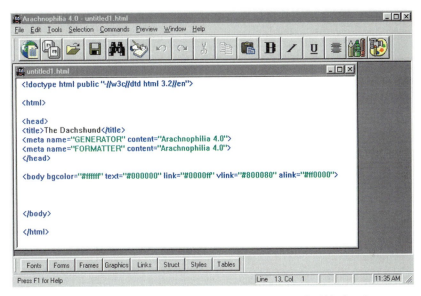

Figure 4.3 Arachnophilia, a Simple HTML Editor (Freeware for Windows)

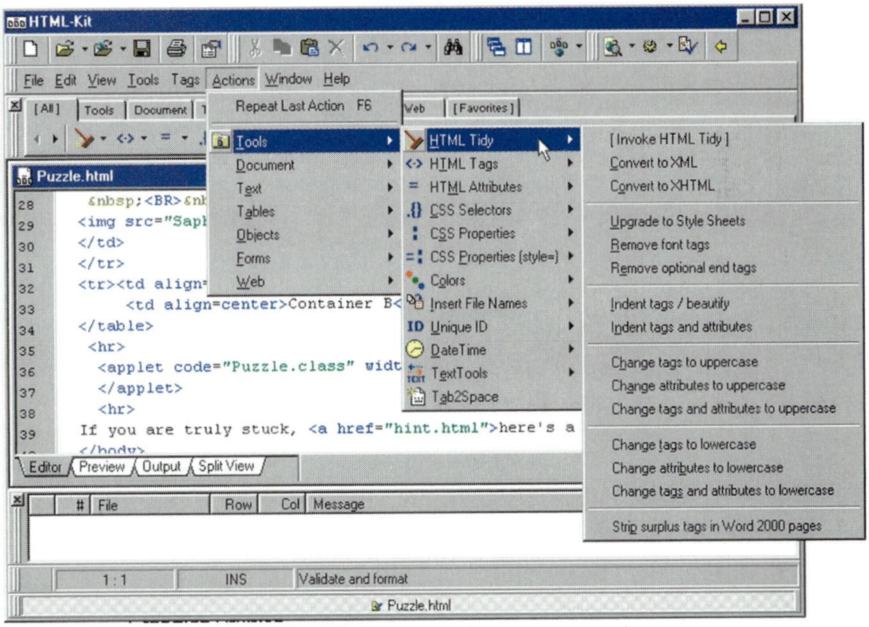

Figure 4.4 HTML-Kit Is an Advanced HTML Editor (Freeware for Windows)

If you inherit an HTML file that is a mess, an **HTML validator** is the right tool to set things right. For example, a freeware validator named Tidy corrects an HTML file where needed and produces a log of errors (such as missing tags or unrecognized tag names) that could not be readily corrected. Tidy also makes a valiant attempt to clean up the horrific HTML generated by certain popular HTML converters (if you've ever looked at the source code for an HTML file generated by Microsoft Word, you know what I'm talking about). Tidy is available for many platforms, including Windows, Macintosh, Linux, and BeOS.

> ☆ **TIP**   **All-in-One Source Code Editor for Programmers**
>
> If you're a programmer, you should know about SynEdit (freeware for Windows). SynEdit is a text and binary file editor with support for 37 programming languages. A good text editor that indents and color-codes source code files can help you correct time-consuming compiler errors. If you work with a lot of languages but don't want to install a big integrated programming environment for each one, SynEdit might be all you need.

◎◎ Graphics Utilities

When you double-click a GIF or JPEG image file, your computer probably launches your default Web browser to view the image. This is fine, but it's a bit like using a sledgehammer to swat a housefly. Browsers are very cumbersome if you want to view more than one image file, especially if you need to search through a directory of image files for the right one. The Open Page command gets very tedious very fast.

If you find yourself doing this more than once a year, forget the browser and install an **image viewer**, a software tool designed for viewing images. Image viewers launch faster than browsers, and give you many welcome features not found in browsers. For example, a good image viewer lets you navigate through all the current image files by pressing a single key. Many viewers also support basic image editing operations such as cropping or saving the image in a different image format. An especially speedy image viewer is IrfanView, which is freeware as long as you use it for noncommercial purposes (see Figure 4.5).

Mac users cannot use IrfanView, but they have their own options. One excellent shareware ($35) option is GraphicConverter by Lemke Software. GraphicConverter offers image editing tools and handles a comprehensive set of file formats, inluding cross-platform conversions (see Figure 4.6).

Although the Web demands GIF and JPEG images, many popular graphics programs work only with `.bmp`, `.tif` (`.tiff`), or `.pct` (`.pict`) images. Some of these programs let you save files in various formats, but they don't always support the format you need. This is when you need an **image converter**, a tool designed strictly for converting images into different formats. Alternatively, you might be able to use a general-purpose utility that offers enough conversion support for your needs. For example, IrfanView can convert all of the most commonly encountered file types.

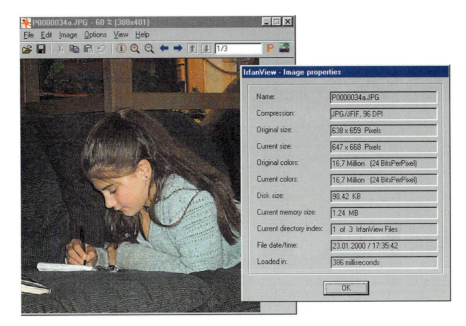

Figure 4.5 The IrfanView Image Viewer (Freeware for Windows)

The GIF format works better with line drawings and artwork whose colors are fixed and flat, whereas the JPEG format is better for images that contain lots of colors with shadings and subtle gradations. Although photographs are usually stored as JPEG files and artwork is usually stored in the GIF format, nothing prevents you from converting a JPEG to a GIF and vice versa. Both formats use compression algorithms to reduce the amount of memory needed to store the image, although they work somewhat differently.

If you use original artwork or photographs on your site, you should have a drawing program, or graphics editor, that lets you edit your images: remove an imperfection with an airbrush, color in a uniform background for a transparent GIF, or maybe play around with special effects. A lot of the fun associated with Web pages relies on a good graphics editor.

If you're a serious artist, you'll want what the professionals use: comprehensive software such as Adobe Photoshop or Adobe Illustrator. But brace yourself—purchasing both of these software titles costs about as much as a new computer.

Happily, there are other options. Corel Painter, for example, is a powerful drawing program for a lot less money. And if you just want to get your toes wet, check out the available freeware before you empty out your bank account. For example, CursorArts ImageForge offers various pen styles, an eyedropper for color sampling, special effects filters, a cloning tool, a fill tool, and more (see Figure 4.7).

Figure 4.6 GraphicConverter (Shareware for the Mac)

◉◉ Link Checkers

Hyperlinks to external URLs become obsolete if you aren't checking them, and this task requires ongoing attention. If you have only 5 or 10 links, you can check them manually every week or two. But if you have more than 10 links, this routine becomes tedious. If you forego the routine, your site will suffer and your visitors will feel neglected or annoyed. It's important to keep your hyperlinks operational and current.

If you maintain a moderately large Web site with more than 100 links and you care about your visitors, you must find a way to have your links checked automatically. There are two ways to go. First, you can subscribe to an application service provider (ASP), which can produce link reports for you weekly or monthly. You don't have to remember to check your links: the service remembers for you. All you have to do is read the reports and fix the links that go stale. These services are very good, but you pay for them as long as you use them, perhaps indefinitely.

If you would like to limit this maintenance expense, it pays to consider the second option: installing a **link checker**, a utility that automates the process of checking your links. Many link checkers are available on the Web. A few are distributed for free, and others are free to try during a trial period. The most sophisticated products (Watchfire's Linkbot Pro 5.0 retails for $395) are designed for professional site administrators and offer sophisticated features for comprehensive site administration. Figure 4.8 shows Xenu's Link Sleuth in action.

Figure 4.7 CursorArts ImageForge (Freeware for Windows)

You can't automate every aspect of hyperlink maintenance. The link checker can only bring problems to your attention, typically in a report summarizing the possible problems found on your site (see Figure 4.9). For each link flagged as questionable or broken, you must decide what to do about it—find a new URL for the original resource or remove the reference.

A good link checker should be easy to use with minimal study and preparation. You need only indicate the location of the Web site by specifying a directory or URL on a Web server, or by listing specific URLs individually. Some link checkers test pages locally before they are installed on a server. Then the link checker collects all the hyperlinks in the target documents and sends requests to all the servers hosting targeted links. If the server replies with a valid Web page, the link passes the test. If an error message is returned, the link is added to the list of problem links. A good link checker associates an error code with each problem link.

Some failures are transient and will disappear if you wait 24 hours. Others are more serious.

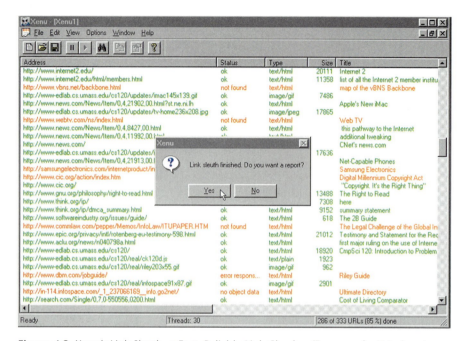

Figure 4.8 Xenu's Link Sleuth, a Fast, Reliable Link Checker (Freeware for Windows)

Figure 4.9 A Link Sleuth Problem Report in HTML Format

Link Checkers

Link maintenance is not as gratifying as Web page construction, but broken links will undermine the value of your site if you let them get away from you. By minimizing the time you spend on routine maintenance, a link checker gives you more time and energy for creative enhancements and major overhauls.

◎◎ Image Mappers

HTML's MAP element splits an image into different regions that respond to mouse events. The different regions are specified by an **image map**. You can create image maps for Web pages using only an image file and a browser. But you must pinpoint all your x-y coordinates, and this is time-consuming and tedious. It's better to use an **image mapper**, a program that helps you create the required HTML code using a simple point-and-click interface.

Image mappers generate an entire MAP element for you based on the information you give them. Let's walk through the process with a freeware Windows image mapper called Dr. Bill's Image Converter and Map Generator. Mapping tools are all similar; after you've seen how one works, you should be able to figure out any of them.

You start by launching the program and selecting Open from the File menu. A directory dialog box appears, where you specify a GIF or JPEG image for the image map.

After the image is loaded, click Edit an HTML Map File in the Options menu. (see Figure 4.10).

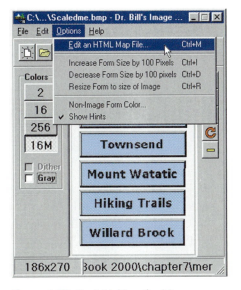

Figure 4.10 Start Making the Map

This command opens a new window with four tabs: Overall Page Design, Map Options, Build an Image Map, and Final HTML Code. We'll work our way across each of these tabs, starting with the leftmost tab (see Figure 4.11). One option here is the check box Create a Complete HTML Page. With this option, the program generates a complete HTML page containing the image map. If you don't check this option, the program generates only the HTML tags for the image map, which you can copy and paste into an existing Web page. The other settings are self-explanatory.

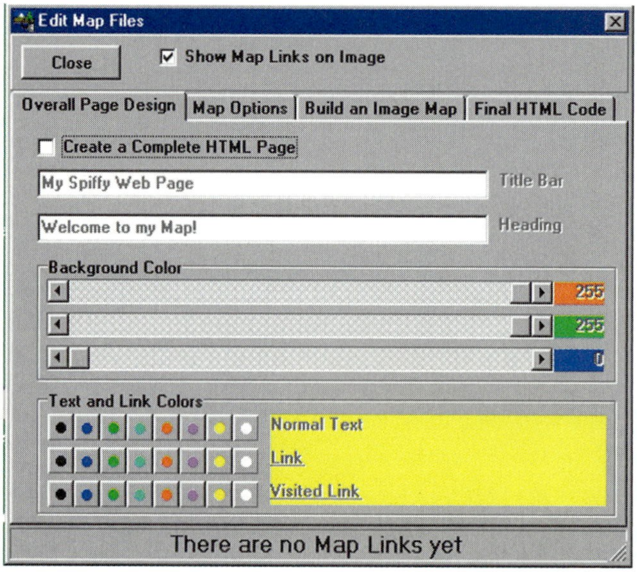

Figure 4.11 You Can Generate a Whole Web Page or an HTML Snippet

Now it's time to map the image map's **hot zones**: those areas of the image that will respond when users sweep over them with a mouse; in this example, the hot zones will be menu buttons. The Build an Image Map tab (third from the left) lets you specify the shapes of the hot zones. In our example, we'll use rectangles for the menu buttons (see Figure 4.12).

Next, go to the image window and use the mouse to mark a rectangular region on the image. To make a rectangle, move the pointer to the upper-left corner of the rectangle. Press and hold the mouse button while dragging the mouse to the lower-right corner. When you release the button, you have specified a rectangle (see Figure 4.13).

When you release the mouse, a third window pops up where you can name a destination for the hot zone you've just defined. You can enter an absolute URL, a relative URL, or a keyword **placeholder** to be replaced with a real URL later. For this example, you use a relative URL.

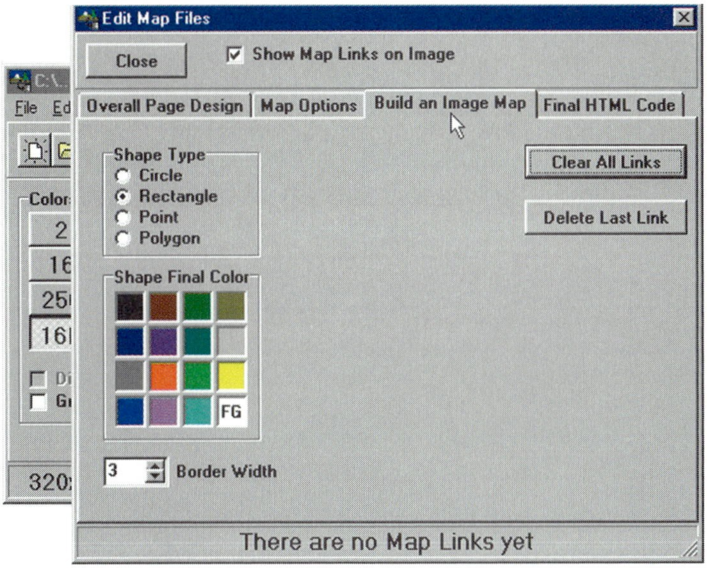

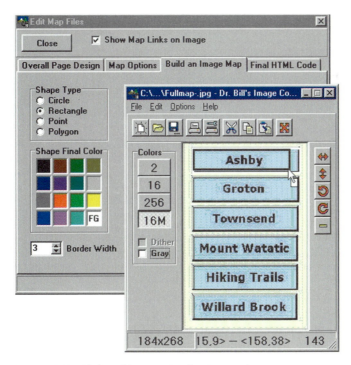

Figure 4.12 Select a Shape for the First Hot Zone

Figure 4.13 Click and Drag to Mark a Rectangle

Now you can return to the Build an Image Map tab and repeat this process for each hot zone in the image map.

At any point, you can visit the Final HTML Code tab to see the HTML tags (see Figure 4.14). When you're finished marking the hot zones, you can save the resulting HTML to a file or copy it to the clipboard for insertion into another HTML file.

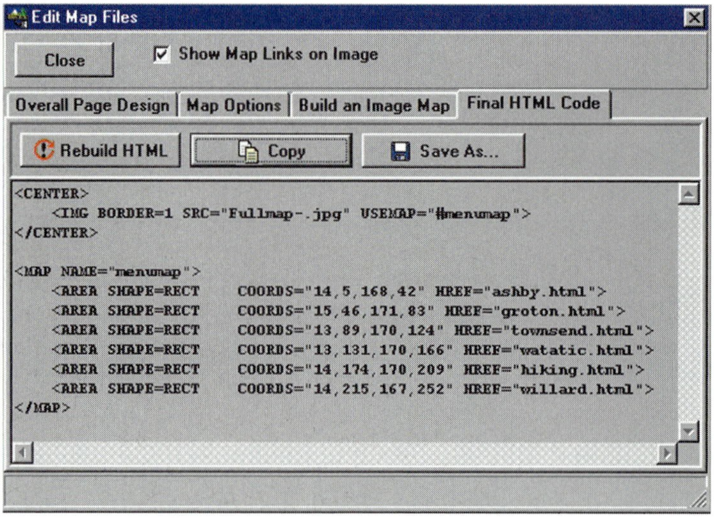

Figure 4.14 Image Mapper Output

★ **SHORTCUT**   An image mapper insulates you from the details associated with MAP and AREA tags. You don't need to know how the tag attributes are used or how the regional coordinates within the area tags will be interpreted. You simply mark the regions of the image, specify the appropriate link locations, and save the final results for reuse.

Special-Purpose Tools

As a Web page designer, you face many tasks, and you can accomplish them with or without special-purpose software tools. Your final results will not betray the methods used; chances are, it all comes down to how much time you have to spend. Good software should make your work easier and faster. If you're doing the same tasks regularly, it pays to find the right set of tools to maximize your productivity.

This section only scratches the surface of the available utilities of interest to Web masters. For example, everyone should have a utility for making transparent GIFs, and everyone should have an image optimizer. Some people can't live without a photo album tool that generates thumbnail sketches, and others need an editor for making animated GIFs. When you work with graphics, it pays to investigate what's available. You might want to subscribe to a software newsletter or mailing list where people discuss software for Web design. The world of software never stands still, so tune in to the grapevine and watch for the software that will make your work easier, faster, or just more fun.

☆ **TIP**   **Looking for a Freeware/Shareware Newsletter?**

Go to `http://www.webattack.com/subscribe/` and subscribe to a weekly newsletter from WebAttack.com. It will keep you up-to-date on the best new freeware for Web design as well as other software categories.

Image Splitters

Navigation panels are usually implemented with image maps, but you can achieve the same effect using only a table if you can split an image into rectangular subsections. This technique, sometimes called a **pseudo image map**, is easy if you have an image splitter.

To start, use a graphics utility to create an image for the navigation panel. Figure 4.15 shows a navigation panel being created with Microsoft Paint.

Figure 4.15 Creating a Navigation Panel with Microsoft Paint (Freeware for Windows)

Next, you divide the image into rectangular subsections so that each part of the image can appear in a separate cell in an HTML table. Figure 4.16 shows Splitz! being used on the navigation bar created in Figure 4.15. In this case, it makes sense to chop the image along the vertical boundaries separating the menu items.

After the cuts have been made, Splitz! generates separate image files for each subsection of the original image (in this example, five image files) and then creates the HTML code for a table. This code reconstructs the original image.

☆ **TIP**   Mac users can find similar utilities. For example, the shareware utility GraphicConverter splits images for pseudo image maps (among other things).

Each image in the table cells can now become a link label for the appropriate hyperlink. As with an image map, clicking on the rectangular regions in the resulting figure takes visitors to the appropriate Web pages (see Figure 4.17).

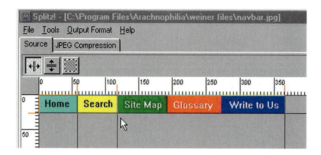

Figure 4.16 Dividing an Image into Pieces with Splitz! (Freeware for Windows)

Figure 4.17 A Pseudo Image Map Using Table Cells

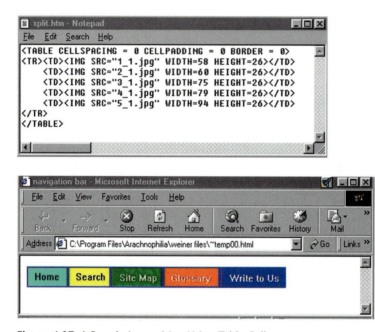

☆ **TIP**   **Piecemeal Image Downloads**

Image splitters can also be used to break up a large image download. If you have an image that requires a lot of bandwidth, use an image splitter to break it into smaller pieces that are then reassembled in an HTML table. When users download the table, the image will appear **piecemeal**, one cell at a time, making the wait a bit less tedious.

Special-Purpose Tools

Button Generators

Image mappers and image splitters make it easy to create image maps and pseudo image maps, but you must first create a suitable image. If you're artistic, you may enjoy creating original art for navigation panels and button sets. You can use a drawing program, or you may want to work offline and then digitize your artwork with a scanner.

But you don't have to be an artist to create professional-looking artwork. **Button generators** are specialized tools that help you craft polished artwork in a matter of seconds. You simply pick a combination of typefaces, colors, and button styles that you like.

Figure 4.18 shows how a user can create buttons using Button Maker. Each button is a combination of features; you select the combinations that produce the look you like. Button Maker even helps you set up button variations for displays that respond to mouseovers. Button generators are terrific time-savers. If you don't want to create your own artwork from scratch, look for a button generator that can give you a look that works for your Web site.

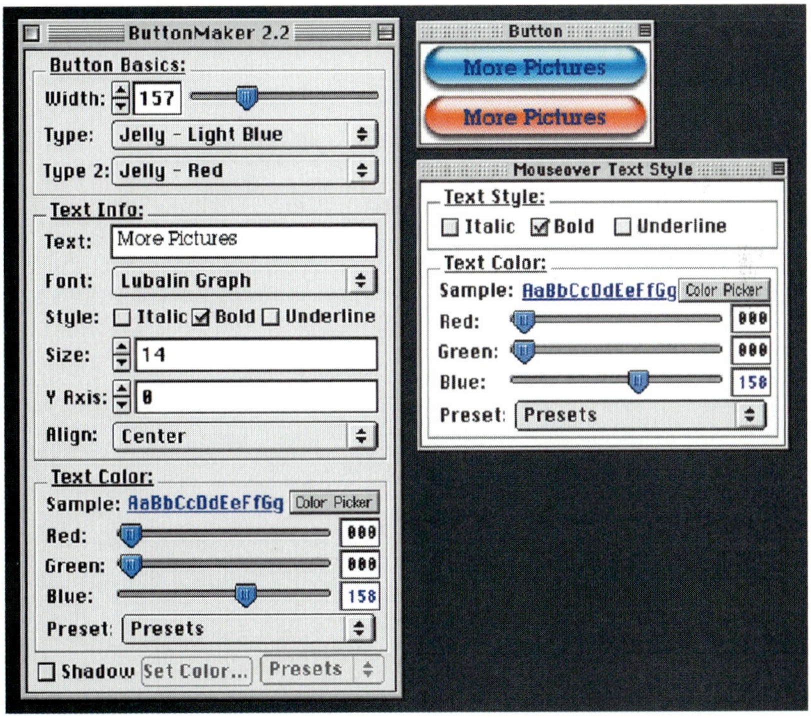

Figure 4.18 Create Button Sets with Button Maker (Freeware for the Mac)

Site Grabbers

Web masters can use a variety of graphics utilities, but many Web-related tasks have nothing to do with graphics. For example, anyone who maintains a large Web site moves a lot of files back and forth. Pages are developed on a local computer and then uploaded to a remote computer, the Web server. Many Web page authors find it helpful to maintain two complete copies of their Web site: one for the Web server and one for local development. Then whenever a page needs to be updated or altered, the local update is moved onto the Web server, and both sites are kept in sync. It sounds simple, but it's easy to slip up and let the two sites fall out of sync.

One way to avoid this problem is to download the entire Web site every so often, especially right before a large updating effort is about to begin. You can easily accomplish this using a site grabbing utility. A **site grabber** downloads files from a Web server, but, unlike an FTP program, the site grabber examines the hyperlinks on each page it downloads to figure out which additional pages should be downloaded. Starting with a root URL, you can tell the site grabber to get only the files in the hyperlinks on that root page (a level 1 retrieval), or you can tell it to download all the pages found in all the hyperlinks in all the level 1 pages (a level 2 retrieval). Figure 4.19 shows a site grabber named SiteSucker downloading files from a small Web site. Specifying a level is one way to limit the number of Web pages returned by the site grabber. Alternatively, you can tell SiteSucker to return all the links on the root page, all the links on all the first-level pages, and so on down the levels—but excluding all links that point to Web pages on other Web servers. This alternative returns all the pages on a given Web site as long as it is all stored on one Web server.

SiteSucker also has a useful localizing feature for your local copy of the Web site. If you mark a check box, SiteSucker reworks the links on the pages so that you can navigate the site offline on your personal computer. As long as the site is self-contained, you won't need an Internet connection to navigate the site. This means that you can explore a Web site while traveling with your laptop even if you have no Internet access.

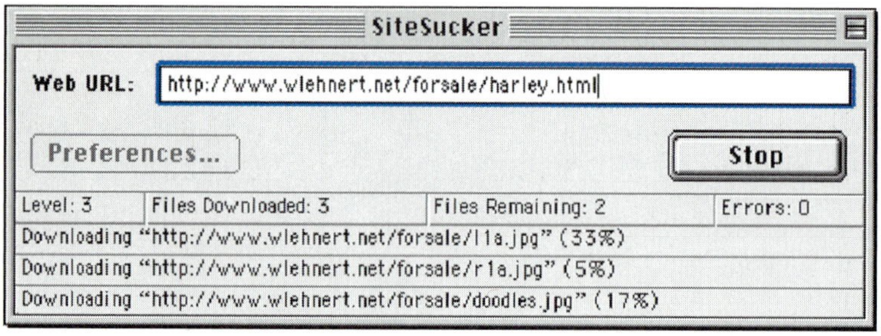

Figure 4.19 Create Button Sets with Button Maker (Freeware for the Mac)

URL Managers

A **URL manager** is a must-have utility that allows you to organize your bookmarks. All browsers have a bookmark facility, but a URL manager gives you additional features. For example, your browser will let you organize your bookmarks in different folders, but you need a URL manager if you want to create pull-down menus for heavily used categories. (Figure 4.20 shows URL Manager, a shareware utility for the Mac.)

URL Manager also lets you consolidate all your Internet addresses. E-mail addresses and FTP addresses for Web servers can be added to your URL folders if you want to keep everything in one place. If your bookmark menus are so long they can't be displayed in a single pull-down menu, you should try a URL manager.

A URL manager is also a necessity for people who work on more than one computer and want to access the same bookmark file on all of them. Updating bookmark files each time you change computers can be tedious. But if you use URL Manager, you can save all your bookmarks to a floppy and move them that way. Updating a URL Manager installation from a floppy is easier than updating your bookmark files directly.

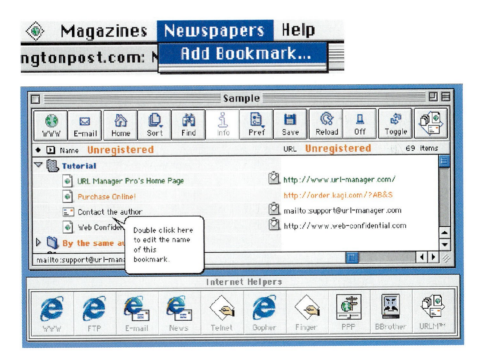

Figure 4.20 Consolidate All Your Web Addresses

⭐ Summary

▷ FTP clients streamline the process of uploading files to Web servers.

▷ HTML editors and validators simplify the creation of healthy HTML files.

▷ If you aren't a professional Web designer, your Web authoring needs can be met with shareware or freeware graphics editors and drawing programs.

▷ Link checking is tedious and time-consuming without help from an automated link checker.

▷ Image mappers make it easy to customize image maps.

▷ Many special-purpose freeware and shareware utilities are available for Web masters and site designers.

⭐ Online References

Arachnophilia
http://www.arachnoid.com/arachnophilia/

ButtonMaker 2.3.1
http://www.mlanier.f2s.com/downloads.php

Dr. Bill's Image Converter and Map Generator
http://www-unix.oit.umass.edu/~verts/software/software.html#IMAGEMAP

GraphicConverter
http://lemkesoft.com/us_gcabout.html

HTML Editors and Associated Tools (mostly for Windows)
http://webdevelopersjournal.com/software/html_editors.html

HTML-Kit
http://www.chami.com/

HTML TIDY
http://www.w3.org/People/Raggett/tidy/

ImageForge
http://www.cursorarts.com/ca_imffw.html

IrfanView
http://www.irfanview.com/

SiteSucker
http://members.aol.com/rcranisky/sitesucker.html

Splitz!
`http://www.b-zone.de/software/splitz.htm`

SynEdit
`http://www.mkidesign.com/syneditinfo.html`

Top HTML Editors for the Mac (suitable for both beginners and professionals)
`http://macworld.zdnet.com/netsmart/features/editorintro.html`

URL Manager
`http://www.url-manager.com/`

WS_FTP LE/WS_FTP PRO
`http://www.ipswitch.com/Purchase/index.html`

Xenu's Link Sleuth
`http://home.snafu.de/tilman/xenulink.html`

☆ Review Questions

1. Name three things that an FTP client can do that a Web browser can't.

2. How do HTML editors help you catch typos and HTML syntax errors as they happen?

3. Explain when a tool like TIDY comes in handy.

4. Microsoft Paint works with only bitmap (`.bmp`) files. Name a freeware utility that can translate an image created by Paint into a GIF file.

5. Compare and contrast Web browsers and image viewers.

6. Why is a link checker preferable to an application service provider that offers a link checking service?

7. What aspect of link checking cannot be automated?

8. Explain how a point-and-click image mapper saves time.

9. Explain how a site grabber might be useful for someone taking a laptop on a cross-country flight.

10. What can a URL manager do that a Web browser can't?

☆ Hands-On Exercises

1. For Windows users. Download and install Twin Color from `http://www.unix.oit.umass.edu/~verts/software/software.html#TWINCOLOR` and find the closest Web-safe color approximations for #4A14A8, #E75830, #C79DA8, #8485A8, #C74FB7, #C712FF, and #E75830. Do you think the program finds an acceptable Web-safe alternative in each case? If it doesn't, do you think you could do better? (Note: The Web-safe colors are all triples made up from the digit pairs 33, 66, 99, CC, and FF.)

2. For Mac users. Go to `http://www.acmetech.com/` and click on the link Products and then the Downloads tab. That will take you to a list of Macintosh downloads, including ColorFinder. Click the Download link. This

will place a file named ColorFinder.hqx on your desktop. Open this with Stuffit Expander. After unpacking, Stuffit Expander will place a file named `ColorFinder.hqx.1` on your desktop. This is an executable installer file. Double-click `ColorFinder.hqx.1`, and you will get a folder named `ColorFinder f.1`. Look inside that folder for the ColorFinder application. Run ColorFinder and use it to find the hexadecimal color code for the blue color at `http://www.tucows.com/`. Is it a Web-safe color? (*Note*: The Web-safe colors are all triples made up from the digit pairs 33, 66, 99, CC, and FF.)

3. For Windows users. Download HTML-Kit at `http://www.chami.com/` and create a simple Web page using it. Compare HTML-Kit to the software you've been using to create Web pages. Which one do you like better? Why?

4. For Mac users. Go to `http://homepage.mac.com/piguet/gif.html` and download the freeware program GIFBuilder 1.0 for creating animated GIFs. Create a simple animated GIF using any images or drawings you have on hand. How hard was it to create your first animated GIF? Do you think this is a utility you may want to use again? Why or why not?

5. Visit `http://download.cnet.com/` and search for freeware image mappers you can run under Windows. How many are there? Check out the user reviews for each one. Do you see one that sounds comparable to Dr. Bill's Image Converter and Map Generator? Which is the most popular shareware image mapper? How much does it cost?

CHAPTER FIVE

SCRIPTS AND APPLETS

Web pages that contain dynamic (visually changing) elements catch the eye and hold attention. If you want to design dynamic elements from scratch, you must learn a programming language (such as JavaScript or Java) and invest a lot of time in your Web pages. Alternatively, you can take advantage of free, ready-to-run programs that you can add to your page. With a little patience and the tips from this chapter, you can dress up your Web pages with professional-looking elements that distinguish your site.

◎ Chapter Objectives

⭐ To understand the difference between JavaScript programs and Java applets, and find out where to find free ones on the Web

⭐ To learn how to install a simple JavaScript script on a Web page

⭐ To see how JavaScript is used to handle hot zones on a Web page

⭐ To find out how to install a simple applet on a Web page

⭐ To see how sophisticated applets can display all kinds of data

◎◎ Scripts and Applets

If you want a quote of the day, a doodle board, a flashy navigation menu, or a graphical special effect, you can easily add one to your Web page using an appropriate **script** (a JavaScript program) or **applet** (a Java program made to work with a Web page). These Web page enhancements are available for free if you know where to look, and you don't have to be a computer programmer to use them. All you need to know is how to edit an HTML file and follow instructions.

To add an applet or a script to a Web page, you need to know how to create a basic Web page. You also need enough understanding of HTML to make manual adjustments to a Web page. If you have some basic familiarity with HTML and you enjoy working with Web pages, this chapter will open up a new world of design possibilities. It's not difficult once you find the right resources, and that part is getting easier all the time.

> ⭐ **WARNING** **This Chapter Assumes Basic Knowledge of HTML**
>
> If you don't know basic HTML, this chapter is not for you. Please read my book *The Web Wizard's Guide to HTML* (Addison-Wesley 2001) or some other introduction to HTML before attempting this chapter.

Scripts and applets are usually distributed as freeware, so it's your responsibility to check for any restrictions that the author has placed on the use of the software. An applet may come with a formal licensing agreement (watch for README files in your file archives), or a lengthy comment at the start of the script might describe any restrictions. Always honor any conditions that apply to scripts and applets found on the Net.

> ⭐ **TIP**   **Scripts and Applets Are Platform-Independent**
>
> You can do everything described in this chapter with both Macs and PCs. All JavaScript scripts and all Java applets can be installed on a Web page using either a Mac or a PC. If you're working on a Mac and you download a script or an applet in a zipped file (`.zip`) archive, Stuffit Expander can unpack it for you.

Using JavaScript Scripts

A JavaScript script is a small fragment of code written specifically to enhance a Web page. **JavaScript** is a programming language that can be used only to enhance Web pages. It's really a **scripting language**, and that means it's used primarily for writing bits of code that can be easily shared, reused, and adapted by many users.

Many JavaScript programs are free; some of them assume programming experience, but many are distributed with instructions for nonprogrammers. Many scripts are excellent and well documented, others are less than perfect but worth the effort, and still others are not worth your time and trouble. After you've installed a few scripts you'll learn to separate the winners from the dogs in a few minutes.

JavaScript enhancements can add a lot to a Web page, but you have to be careful because different browsers support slightly different versions of JavaScript. This means that a JavaScript program may run correctly under only one browser. It's always good to test your script with both Netscape Navigator and Internet Explorer in case the script relies on browser-specific features.

When professionals add JavaScript to a Web page, they test the page extensively not only with both browsers but also with different versions of both browsers. To attain uniform page displays, you may need to add two scripts to the same page: one for Navigator and one for Explorer. You add a test condition that asks the current browser to identify itself, and that determines which script will be executed.

⭐ **SHORTCUT**   In spite of your efforts, you may still see some differences when the same page is viewed with different browsers. One approach is to insert a warning to your visitors (as in, "This page is best viewed with Netscape Navigator"). Visitors running the other browser won't be thrilled, but at least they've been warned.

You can learn JavaScript by playing around with lots of scripts and learning from examples. But if you've never worked with a programming language before, learning from examples will be difficult. If you've done a little programming in any other language, you'll find it easier, although learning from examples always leaves some gaps. But JavaScript is a lot of fun, and when you learn from examples you can pick and choose the ones that interest you. And you can see the results of your labors with any browser. If you like what you see, you can post it for all the world to see.

⭐ **TIP**   **Scripting Languages**

There are many scripting languages, including JavaScript, HyperCard, AppleScript, Jscript, and VBScript. Some of these scripting languages are designed specifically for Web pages, and others (HyperCard and AppleScript) have nothing to do with the Web. JavaScript is the most popular scripting language for the Web, and most browsers know how to read JavaScript inserts in an HTML file (as long as the JavaScript preference setting is enabled).

You usually acquire scripts in one of three ways. Some scripts are customized for you by a Web server at an interactive Web site where you're asked a few questions first. See htmlGEAR for some useful examples of server-side script customization.

Other scripts are made available as software downloads. You download and install an **authoring tool** (often called a **wizard**) that helps you customize your script on your own computer. Authoring tools are generally found in software archives that specialize in Web construction tools. Visit HTML Goodies to find authoring tools that produce customized scripts.

Finally, some scripts are distributed as simple **cut-and-paste text files** that contain baseline code for a script along with instructions for simple modifications. Some cut-and-paste scripts are well documented and easy for anyone to install. Others offer minimal assistance and are more appropriate for experienced programmers. Visit JavaScript Search for a large collection of cut-and-paste scripts.

☆ **WARNING**   How Risky Are Free JavaScript Downloads?

Whenever you run an executable file on your personal computer, there is some risk, and JavaScript programs *can* be dangerous. For example, a JavaScript program could send personal information from your computer to a remote computer without your knowledge. If you can read and understand the source code you're running, you can assess your risks. But if you simply cut and paste, there is a chance that you could install something deceptive and malicious. If you want to err on the side of caution, restrict yourself to scripts from highly reputable Web sites, such as sites associated with textbooks and major publishing houses. Or learn a little JavaScript. It doesn't take a master programmer to see whether a script is up to something fishy.

Using Java Applets

Java is a general programming language with powerful graphical capabilities. Java is not restricted to Web programming, but it can be used to create interactive Web pages. A **Java applet** is a piece of Java code that is added to an HTML file and executed when a Web browser displays the page. Some of the most stunning visual effects seen on Web pages are produced by applets. More utilitarian applets can be customized in so many ways that they come with what amounts to a user manual. Many applets are specifically designed for non-programmers who want to enhance their Web pages.

Many excellent applets are given away, although some of the more complicated ones can cost $100 or more. Applets are written in Java, but you don't need to know anything about Java to install an applet on your own Web page. In fact, a well-documented applet is usually easier to install and customize than a well-documented script. Many collections of free applets can be found on the Web. If you have the time, it's fun to peruse applet libraries and see what's available. You'll be surprised by what you can find for free.

Applets can be found at **applet archives** (sites similar to software clearinghouses). Each applet is stored in one or more binary files with a `.class` file extension. These files contain the executable code for the applet. Because all `.class` files are binary, you can't open and read them. They can be executed only by a Java-enabled Web browser.

☆ **TIP**   How Risky Are Free Java Applets?

In general, executable files always entail risks, and executables that are distributed without source code files (for example, as `.class` files) should make anyone nervous. But Java applets and the browsers that support them are constrained by strict limitations designed to protect your security online. In particular, Java applets cannot read or write to files. This means that applets cannot alter or delete files on your hard drive, nor can they send copies of your personal files to a remote computer. For this reason, Java applets are much safer than JavaScript scripts. If an applet does something you weren't expecting, at least it won't be destructive like a computer virus.

Special-Effects Scripts

Many visual effects can be achieved with easy-to-install scripts. Most of these special effects are dynamic: Elements of the image move or **morph** (change appearance). For that reason, it's difficult to do justice to the more arresting examples in print.

We'll look at an example that bounces an image around inside a browser window. To achieve this effect, all you need is a Web page (for the background), an image (to bounce in the foreground), and a script named PicturePong. For the foreground image, let's use an animated creature that waves its arms up and down while gently bouncing up and down (see Figure 5.1 and use your imagination).

Figure 5.1 A Bouncing Animated GIF

For background, we'll use a Web page that describes the PicturePong script. The easiest script installations are documented in one or two sentences. Figure 5.2 explains how to install PicturePong (see the bullet under Configuration) and shows how the animated GIF moves across the page. (Again, you have to use your imagination, or visit `http://www.24fun.com` to see the script in action.)

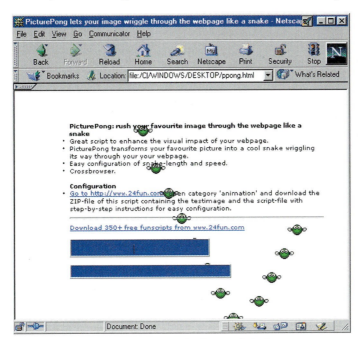

Figure 5.2 The PicturePong Script in (Stopped) Action

More detailed instructions for PicturePong (from `www.24fun.com`) read as follows:

⭐ *Download the script as ZIP-file, extract the HTML-file and the testimage and save them both into the same folder.*

⭐ *Open the HTML-file, go the head-section of the script and configure the image-url, speed and snake-length at the top of the script.*

⭐ *Go to the body-section of the HTML-file and delete the div-block with the id "deletethisblock".*

The key instructions are "go [to] the head-section of the script and configure the image-url, speed and snake-length at the top of the script." This refers to three variable settings at the start of the script. You can see the script by looking at the source code behind the HTML file in the zipped archive. The full script is too long to reproduce here, but the beginning of the script looks like this:

```
// URL of your image. Attention: big images will slow
// down the script
var your_image="testimage86.gif"        the image-url

// speed
var tempo=40        the speed

// average horizontal distance between the images
var stepx=20

// average vertical distance between the images
var stepy=20

// number of images
var numberofimages=12        the snake-length
```

⭐ **TIP   Script Comments**

When you look at the source code, pay attention to comment lines. Short comments are signaled by two forward slashes ("//") at the start of the line. Longer, multiple-line comments may be placed between the start comment string ("/*") and the end comment string ("*/"). Script authors use comments to document their code, explain installation options, include warnings, and make helpful suggestions.

From this code you can see that five variables can be modified in addition to the image URL (called `your_image`), the speed (called `tempo`), and the snake length (called `numberofimages`). To alter the behavior of the script, you can modify any of these variable values, experimenting with different values to see how they affect the display.

The most important variable is the image URL, which must be modified if you want to use your image. You don't need to change the other variable values if you're happy with the **default** (given) settings. After you've edited the script as needed, you can review the resulting Web page. If you like what you see, you can upload it (along with the foreground image) to a Web server.

PicturePong contains these comments:

```
// IMPORTANT:
// If you add this script to a script-library or a
// script-archive you have to insert a link to
// http://www.24fun.com right into the webpage where the
// script will be displayed.
```

This means that the PicturePong script is a type of **linkware**: software that's freely distributed as long as you include a hyperlink to a designated URL to acknowledge the source. According to these instructions, PicturePong can be used on a personal Web page without a link to `24fun.com`, but if you want to redistribute it in a collection of scripts you must include a link to PicturePong's home page.

☆**TIP**   **Working with `.js` Files**

Sometimes a lengthy JavaScript program will be stored inside a separate `.js` file instead of an HTML file. Then the HTML file references the `.js` file so that the browser can find the script. (For details on how this is done, check the sample HTML file or the installation instructions that come with the download.) If you download a script that includes a `.js` file and you want to modify some settings, you may need to open the `.js` file. Don't worry—you can always open any `.js` file with a text editor.

◎◎ Mouseover Scripts

This section presents a JavaScript example that requires more extensive modifications. This situation is typical with the more complicated scripts you find on the Web, which assume some familiarity with JavaScript. If this walk-through seems a little hard to follow, it's because I can't really hope to give you a systematic introduction to JavaScript in a few pages. But I'll try to give you a taste of what to expect when a script is not prepackaged for beginners.

The example—a dynamic mouseover—is used extensively throughout the Web. A **mouseover** happens when the user sweeps the mouse over a region on a Web page that has been programmed to respond to the mouse. As explained in Chapter Four, a region that responds to mouseovers is called a **hot zone**. As soon as the mouse enters a hot zone, something happens. Usually, something new appears on the Web page: A comment box pops up, a button changes color, or an image is transformed. This element makes a Web page visually interactive and more fun for people to explore. Because there are so many different things you can do with them, mouseovers are one of the most versatile features you can add to a Web page.

☆**WARNING** **Fasten Your Seat Belt**

The example in this section will be easier to follow if you've done a little computer programming. If you have never worked with a programming language and you get bogged down with this mouseover example, skip it and move to the next section. You don't need to understand this example to understand the rest of the chapter.

Here, I present a complete mouseover script that you can add to your Web pages, and I explain it so that you can modify it for any Web page with any number of hot zones. I go into more detail than you normally see in script installation directions, but less detail than you would need if you were writing this script from scratch. Understanding this script will make it possible for you to adapt it to your needs. The more scripts you work with, the easier these adaptations will be.

> ⭐ **TIP** **First Things First**
>
> To understand the installation of this mouseover script, you first need some familiarity with client-side image maps. I don't go into the details of image maps here, but you can learn all about them on the Net. For example, HTML Goodies has a good image map tutorial.

A mouseover script is not the simplest script available, nor is it the most complicated. If you understand this example well enough to use it, you should be able to work with most of the scripts you'll find online.

Before you look at the JavaScript behind a button panel mouseover, think about the images working behind the scenes. For each button on the navigational menu, you need at least two images: a default button when no mouse activity is present, and a highlighted button when the mouse is inside the button's hot zone (see Figure 5.3). Because these images are almost identical, the browser can **swap** them (exchange one for another) on the Web page and make it look as if a single image is magically changing before our eyes. Most browsers can swap images so smoothly that there is no flickering or any other indication of the exchange.

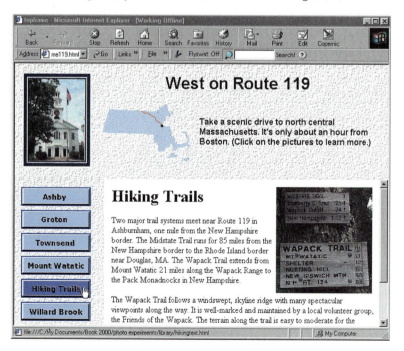

Figure 5.3 A Mouseover for a Button Panel

> ☆ **TIP**   **You Can Create Your Own Button Sets**
>
> If you're making your own image files, start with one default file for the entire menu and then use a drawing program to modify the original to create the mouseover variations. A simple bitmap image editor, such as Windows Paint, is all you need if you're patient. Try to make as few changes as possible. Keep all the buttons lined up in exactly the same locations in all your image files; otherwise, users will see the buttons shift when the images are swapped. Rather than redraw entire buttons, keep the original button outline and text label, and use a fill operation to change the background color. Use the same operation to change the text color if you want the mouseover to highlight text.

Figure 5.4 shows two variations on a default button panel: a highlighted button for mouseovers and a depressed button for mouse clicks. The difference between the two versions lies in the shadows bordering the button's face. To show a raised 3-D surface and a depressed surface, you reverse the light and dark edges surrounding the face of the image. Wider edges make the effect more prominent, and narrow edges keep it subtle.

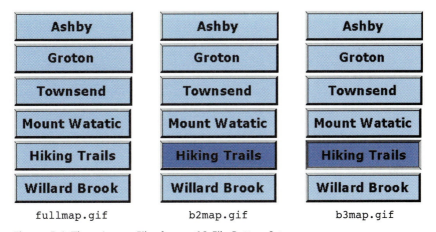

Figure 5.4 Three Image Files from a 13-File Button Set

This button set contains 13 files: one default display (the leftmost panel in Figure 5.4) and two variations on the default for each of six separate buttons (Figure 5.4 shows the two Hiking Trails variations). Working with the whole menu at once, as shown here, makes the image layout easier because you need only swap the one image repeatedly. But this is not a good approach if you ever need to modify your menu. Any change to the button set in Figure 5.4 will require you to remake all 13 files. To make these revisions as painless as possible, create a separate default file for each button and display the buttons using separate button files inside individual table cells. The file swaps inside the script are a little more complicated, but it's not difficult, and you'll have less work when it's time to add a new button or replace an old one.

The hot zones to be used for the mouseovers must first be specified in an image map. After the image map has been made, you simply attach instructions to each hot zone, specifying what should happen when the mouse enters and leaves the region. In other words, you specify which image file should be loaded when a mouseover occurs (the mouse enters a specific hot zone) and which image file should be loaded when a **mouseout** occurs (the mouse leaves the hot zone). For the hot zones to respond to mouse clicks as well as mouseovers, you also need separate instructions for mouse clicks.

The script that implements the image swaps relies on a JavaScript procedure that lets you load any image into any image location on the existing page. The page in Figure 5.3 consists of multiple frames, but we need to modify the HTML file for the menu frame. In this example, the menu page contains only a single image location (one `IMG` tag for the default button panel), so it's not hard to figure out which image should be replaced for each mouseover. If we were using a separate image file for each button, we would need to number the image locations (six locations for six buttons) to keep them all straight.

Image swapping is easy when you understand how JavaScript looks at an HTML file. Each `IMG` tag in an HTML file is considered to be a fixed object (an **object instance**, in the language of object-oriented programming). Although the object itself is fixed, its attributes can be changed by a script. In particular, the `SRC` attribute of any `IMG` object can be changed, and this is all we need for an image swap. JavaScript also makes it easy to specify different `IMG` objects when a page contains more than one. JavaScript counts the `IMG` tags and assigns each one an integer based on its location in the HTML file (the first `IMG` tag, the second `IMG` tag, etc.).

Even though this example involves only one image object, we'll use a swapping script that also works on pages having multiple images. We'll tune it for a Web page with one image. To refer to an image on a Web page you need to understand how JavaScript counts things. Although humans like to count starting from 1 (1, 2, 3, and so on), JavaScript uses a counting convention that starts from 0 (0, 1, 2, 3, and so on). So as far as your script is concerned, the first image in an HTML file is always image 0, the second image is image 1, the third is image 2, and so forth. We have only one `IMG` tag in your menu file, so the button panel is always image 0.

You also need to know how to refer to the various image files in a button set. JavaScript handles this by creating multiple instances of image objects. Each image object is assigned a `SRC` attribute much like the `IMG` tag and `SRC` attribute in HTML, but the syntax for describing an image object in a script is a little different from the syntax for images in HTML. Remember, HTML and JavaScript are two different things, even though they both allow us to manipulate the same sorts of entities (such as images from files). One representational system applies to HTML, and a different representational system is used for JavaScript programs. When an HTML page contains a script, it is always inside a `SCRIPT` tag. The text inside a `SCRIPT` tag may look something like HTML, but it's not! The text inside a `SCRIPT` tag is always a computer program—in this case, a JavaScript program.

The script consists of two parts: (1) a set of object instances that specify all the image files in the button set and (2) the procedure that actually makes the swaps. The full script for this example would need 13 image instances to cover the 13 button files, but I show only the three image instances needed to handle the Hiking Trails button.

In JavaScript you can assign a name to each image object so that you can call them from elsewhere in the script. This means that you can change the SRC value of the IMG object on demand, and that's how you'll make the image swaps when the mouse enters or leaves a hot zone.

Figure 5.5 shows a complete script for handling mouseovers and mouse clicks. The script is found inside the <SCRIPT></SCRIPT> tag pair, which goes inside the page's HEAD element. The script creates three image objects and defines a procedure named ChangeTo. This procedure accepts two bits of input: (1) the location (specified by number) of an image on the current Web page and (2) an instance of an image object defined inside the script. When you execute this procedure, it loads the graphics file for the script's image object into the specified image on the Web page. In other words, it performs an image swap.

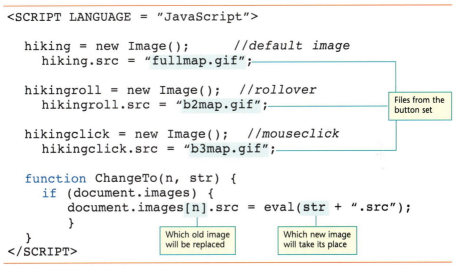

```
<SCRIPT LANGUAGE = "JavaScript">

  hiking = new Image();       //default image
     hiking.src = "fullmap.gif";

  hikingroll = new Image();   //rollover
     hikingroll.src = "b2map.gif";

  hikingclick = new Image();   //mouseclick
     hikingclick.src = "b3map.gif";

  function ChangeTo(n, str) {
     if (document.images) {
        document.images[n].src = eval(str + ".src");
        }
     }
</SCRIPT>
```

Files from the button set

Which old image will be replaced

Which new image will take its place

Figure 5.5 A Script for Image Swaps

Don't get bogged down in the strange-looking JavaScript syntax. You don't need to reproduce this script from scratch. It's enough to understand roughly what's going on. Figure 5.6 may help.

Create an instance of an image object and name it "hiking."

Set the SRC attribute of the hiking object to "fullmap.gif."

```
<SCRIPT LANGUAGE = "JavaScript">

hiking = new Image();        //default image
    hiking.src = "fullmap.gif";

hikingroll = new Image();  //rollover
    hikingroll.src = "b2map.gif";

hikingclick = new Image();  //mouseclick
    hikingclick.src = "b3map.gif";

function ChangeTo(n, str) {
    if (document.images) {
        document.images[n].src = eval(str + ".src");
    }
}
</SCRIPT>
```

Set the SRC attribute of the *n*th image object in the Web page to...

...the value of the SRC attribute in the image object that was input to this procedure.

Figure 5.6 JavaScript Syntax Demystified

This script creates a procedure for swapping images, and now you must specify when the procedure should run and with what input. Having a definition of the `ChangeTo` procedure is great, but now you need more instructions that explain how `ChangeTo` will be used. You'll add those instructions to the image map (see below). Inside each of the `AREA` tags within the `MAP` element you add new attributes named `mouseOver`, `MouseOut`, `MouseDown`, and `mouseUp`. The value of these attributes is a call to the procedure `ChangeTo`. Each procedure call specifies which image location should be swapped (it's always the same one) and which image object should be inserted (it's always one of the three image objects named in the script).

```
<body background="birdbg.jpg">
<img src="fullmap.gif" width="181" height="267"
usemap="#menumap">
<map name="menumap">
   <area shape=RECT coords="14,5,168,42"
href="ashby.html">
   <area shape=RECT coords="15,46,171,83"
href="groton.html">
   <area shape=RECT coords="13,89,170,124"
href="townsend.html">
   <area shape=RECT coords="13,131,170,166"
href="watatic.html">
   <area shape=RECT coords="14,174,170,209"
href="hikingtext.html"
      target="text"
      onMouseOver="ChangeTo(0,'hikingroll')"
      onMouseOut="ChangeTo(0,'hiking')"
```

```
onMouseDown="ChangeTo(0,'hikingclick')"
onMouseUp="ChangeTo(0,'hikingroll')">
<area shape=RECT coords="14,215,167,252"
href="willard.html">
</map>
</body>
```

> ⭐ **TIP**   **JavaScript and Mouse Events**
>
> This example uses four mouse events: onmouseover, onmouseout, onmousedown, and onmouseup. You can use others in your AREA tags if you want to experiment with more dynamic effects. onclick is recognized when a mousedown event is immediately followed by a mouseup event. ondbclick is a fast double-click. onmousemove is recognized when the mouse moves inside the hot zone. onkeydown is recognized when a key on the keyboard is pressed. onkeyup is a key being released, and onkeypress is a key being pressed and then quickly released (analogous to onclick for the mouse).

That's all there is to it. If you can make sense of these code snippets, you should understand this script well enough to plug it in to a Web page of your own and adjust it to fit your own image-swapping needs. To adapt this script to handle all six buttons, you add three new image objects (one for each of the other buttons) along with appropriate ChangeTo instructions inside each of the AREA tags for each of the button hot zones.

JavaScript gives your Web page the power to respond to many different types of mouse events, and image maps give you the freedom to define behaviors for various parts of your Web page.

Safety Issues with JavaScript

If you worry about computer viruses, you may be wondering whether JavaScript has a dark side. After all, these scripts are executable computer programs, and they're being executed on your computer whenever you visit a Web page that contains JavaScript. You are right to wonder. Computer programmers worried a lot about this when browsers first began to support JavaScript. Happily, many of those worried programmers were responsible for making JavaScript safe.

What are the risks? Thanks to safeguards built into JavaScript, no one has been able to embed a true virus in a JavaScript program. But read on. It is possible to create a malicious JavaScript program. For example, an ill-tempered programmer could create a script designed to open a thousand browser windows as soon as you visit a booby-trapped Web page. Opening this many windows would crash your system.

What can you do to be safe? One option is to change your browser's preference setting to disable all scripting languages. For Netscape Navigator, go to the Advanced preference settings and uncheck the check box for Enable JavaScript; for Internet Explorer, go to Internet Options, select the Security tab, highlight Internet, press the Custom Level button, and activate the Disable Active Scripting radio button. But this will cost you. You'll miss out on a lot of what the Web has to offer, including all e-commerce transactions, all user-customizable sites, and all sites that require user registrations (not to mention all the nifty interactive visual effects).

For most people, the level of risk associated with JavaScript is acceptable. If you're willing to walk out of your house even though some crazy person could drive by and take a shot at you, you really shouldn't worry about JavaScript. For most of us, these are simply risks we are willing to live with.

Where to Find Script Libraries

Any general search engine will give you pointers if you enter the query "JavaScripts." Here's a sampling of what's out there (in alphabetical order). The sites marked with three asterisks are especially good for beginners.

☆   `*** http://JavaScript.internet.com/`

☆   `http://www.24fun.ch/`

☆   `http://www.developer.com/downloads/code/`
      `JavaScripts.html`

☆   `*** http://www.essex1.com/people/timothy/js-index.htm`

☆   `http://www.exeat.com/`

☆   `http://www.freecode.com/`

☆   `http://www.geocities.com/SiliconValley/7116/`

☆   `http://www.infohiway.com/JavaScript/indexf.htm`

☆   `http://www.JavaScripts.com/`

☆   `http://www.JavaScriptsearch.com/`

☆   `http://www.js-planet.com/`

☆   `http://www.scripts.com/JavaScript/`

☆   `http://www.thefreesite.com/freejava.htm`

☆   `http://www.webmonkey.com/`

☆   `*** http://www.wsabstract.com/`

Keep in mind that some scripts are simpler than others, and some have better documentation than others. If you're a beginner, you'll want to look for simpler ones that are well explained. It won't hurt to take a peek at something complicated just for kicks, but you shouldn't expect to understand it. You should also know that there is usually more than one way to skin a cat with JavaScript. If one approach makes no sense to you, keep looking until you find one that does. Don't forget that some approaches may work for only one browser, so pay close attention to comments about browser compatibility.

Learning to Write Your Own Scripts

You can learn JavaScript on the Web, or you can buy a book. Here are a few good online tutorials to get you started.

⭐ 30-step JavaScript Primer, by Joe Burns:
`http://www.htmlgoodies.com/primers/`

⭐ Voodoo's Introduction to JavaScript, by Stefan Koch:
`http://rummelplatz.uni-mannheim.de/~skoch/js/`
`tutorial.htm`

⭐ Thau's JavaScript Tutorial (in five lessons):
`http://hotwired.lycos.com/webmonkey/98/03/index0a.html`

⭐ A collection of short JavaScript tutorials on specific topics:
`http://www.wsabstract.com/javaindex.shtml`

⭐ Free JavaScript Learning Center (a 14-lesson tutorial):
`http://www.crays.com/learn/`

⭐ JavaScript for Beginners:
`http://www.builder.com/Programming/JavaScript/`

I'd be remiss if I failed to mention *The Web Wizard's Guide to JavaScript*, by Steven Estrella.

Other JavaScript Tasks

JavaScript scripts aren't limited to creating cosmetic special effects. They're also useful for a variety of practical processing tasks. For example, a JavaScript script can check Web form entries before form data is sent back to the server. Have you ever filled out a form and skipped a required entry? Chances are, you were told to go back and fill in the missing entry. This correction was probably generated by a special-purpose script, a **form verification** script, without any data going out over the Net.

JavaScript can also be used to place cookies on your hard drive, read cookies that are already there, and personalize your experience on the Web accordingly.

Interestingly, utilities that block cookies typically work by inserting a script (written in JavaScript) into every Web page you download—*after* they're retrieved from a Web server and *before* they're rendered by your Web browser. The script inserted by the cookie blocker overrides the script inserted by the Web page author, and the cookie blocker wins.

JavaScript is a versatile language, and programmers are exploring new applications for it all the time. If you want to stay on top of the latest developments, subscribe to a weekly newsletter affiliated with one of the larger JavaScript clearinghouses.

If you've tried your hand at installing some JavaScript scripts, you may have concluded that JavaScript is too time-consuming for you. It is time-consuming, but some people have the time and enjoy the challenge. Others can't be bothered and feel frustrated when things don't work perfectly on the first try. Either way, you'll be happy to hear that Java applets are easier to install than JavaScript scripts. Read on.

◎◎ Special-Effects Applets

A Java applet is similar to a JavaScript script insofar as it is a small program that is attached to a Web page and executed by the client when the page is retrieved from its server. But an applet is different in terms of the requirements on the client side. A Java applet must be executed by a **JVM (Java Virtual Machine)**, which works alongside the browser to execute the applet when the page containing it is downloaded. You may have noticed that your browser takes a long time to load certain pages the first time you visit them during a browsing session. A likely cause is that your browser is loading Java in order to execute an applet on the page being downloaded. When a browser loads Java, it launches the JVM, a substantial application in its own right. After the JVM is running, it stays alive in the background so that you won't have to launch it again unless you restart your browser.

Java is unique among programming languages because it was designed to be platform-independent. In theory, the same Java program will run without adjustments on computers running Windows, UNIX, or the Macintosh operating system. Each platform needs its own JVM, but after the JVM has been installed, any Java program can be run on that computer. Although platform independence has not been completely realized, applets benefit from the attempt: The same applet can be run on any Java-enabled browser under any operating system. A given applet may not produce identical displays or behavior on all computers, but browser compatibility is much less of a problem for applets than it is for JavaScript scripts.

Safety Issues with Applets

Again, the question of safety should occur to you. You're downloading executable code from an unknown source. How much risk is there?

In general, applets are safer than JavaScript scripts because applets cannot read or write to any files (not even cookie files). Those restrictions make it impossible to embed a computer virus inside an applet. However, applets can send information back to the server that sent the applet. So whenever you interact with an applet, you may be sending information to a Web server (with or without your knowledge). If an applet asks you for personal information, the usual privacy concerns apply. But in general, applets pose less risk than JavaScript scripts, so if you're willing to run a JavaScript-enabled browser, you should not be scared of a Java-enabled browser.

Compared with JavaScript scripts, it's easier to add Java applets to a Web page because they're self-contained. Unlike JavaScript scripts, each applet is packaged in what amounts to a locked box that cannot be opened, inspected, or modified. You take what you get, you plug it in, and it either works or it doesn't. You can't modify an applet by going into its code and fussing with lines here and there. In fact, you can't even see the source code unless the author has chosen to distribute it alongside the applet for educational purposes. (Some applets are distributed with source code, but it's intended for Java programmers and isn't explained.)

Adding Visual Effects

Let's look at some sample applets so that you can see how easy it is to install an applet written by someone else on your Web page. The simplest applets apply special effects to underlying GIF or JPG image files. With the right applet, you can add falling snowflakes to a winter scene or add ripples to the water in a photograph of a lake. You can make a flag wave or add a moving magnifying glass to an image. These are only a few of the special effects you can add.

Figure 5.7 shows an applet called alcsnow. The image on the left is an undoctored photograph displayed by an `IMG` element. The image on the right is the same photograph displayed inside the alcsnow applet. When you view this applet with a Web browser, the snowflakes fall to the ground in a never-ending snowstorm. Figure 5.7 can't show this motion. To get the full effect, go to `http://www.webmoments.com/java/` and check out the ALC Snow link.

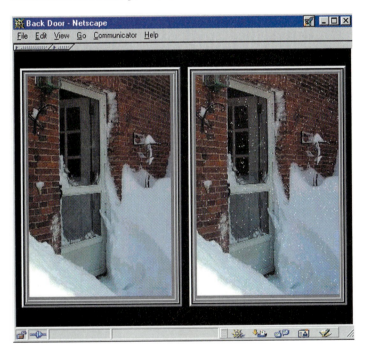

Figure 5.7 Adding Falling Snow to a Winter Scene

To add the alcsnow applet to a Web page, you insert the following code where you would normally insert an IMG tag:

```
<applet code="alcsnow" width="222" height="334">
<param name="grph" value="door2.jpg">
<param name="snows" value="500">
<param name="threadsleep" value="50">
</applet>
```

To make the applet work for your image, you would substitute the name of your image file in place of `door2.jpg`, using the correct width and height of your image file.

You can download this applet from `http://www.webmoments.com/java/alcsnow.htm`, where you can also find complete installation instructions. To make the applet run, you place the `alcsnow.class` file in the same directory as the HTML file that contains the applet tag pair and the image file to be altered.

Some special effects applets are interactive: Viewers can play with the image to alter its appearance. **Morphing** applets, which deform images, are a popular choice, especially when loaded with photographs of teachers, presidential candidates, or supermodels. Figure 5.8 shows how a Web visitor can transform a dachshund into a pumped-up wunderhund using a few drag-and-drop operations. Each drag and drop deforms the image by stretching a region from the dragged location toward the dropped location. (No animals were harmed to achieve this special effect, which was achieved with an applet called AlexWarp.)

Figure 5.8 Pump Up Your Pet with an Applet

Here's the code for the applet:

```
<applet code="AlexWarp" width="525" height="365">
<param name="image" value="donut.jpg">
</applet>
```

The AlexWarp applet is available at `http://www.webmoments.com`.

> ⭐ **WARNING** Before you install an applet on a Web page, read the documentation for descriptions of the param tags. Some parameters are self-explanatory, and others may require some explanation. If you want to modify a param tag, change only the `value` of the `value` attribute ("`donut.jpg`" in the example). Never change the value of the `name` attribute ("image" in the example). Also, whenever a file name is needed for a param value, make sure the file is located in the same subdirectory as the Web page with the applet tag (unless you want to include a directory path in addition to the file name).

> ⭐ **TIP   The Applet Tag Has Been Deprecated**
>
> The APPLET tag has been **deprecated** (discontinued) in HTML 4.0 and XHTML 1.0. This means that Web browsers will continue to support the APPLET tag for some indefinite period, but the tag is old and has been superseded by a newer OBJECT tag. Either tag will work, although the OBJECT tag is preferable if you want your Web pages to look up-to-date.

Sometimes an applet being distributed for general use requires additional support files for its parameter values. You may need to supply your own support files, or they may be packaged with the applet. Downloadable applets are generally stored in file archives so that you'll receive everything you need in one download. Always look for a `readme.txt` file, which may contain important installation instructions.

How to Install an Applet

Typically, you install an applet in seven steps.

1. Download and unpack the applet.
2. Read all available documentation.
3. Insert the required HTML snippet into your Web page.
4. Modify param values as needed.
5. Upload your Web page to the server.
6. Upload the required `.class` file(s) to the server.
7. Upload any required support files to the server.

Finding Applets on the Web

I can't list all the sites worth mentioning, but here's a starter set. You can add to it as you discover more.

⭐ `http://javaboutique.internet.com/` (one of the major sites)

⭐ `http://freewarejava.com/` (another large site)

★ `http://wsabstract.com/java/` (another large site)

★ `http://www.javapowered.com/` (nice stuff; visit the showcase and check out the newest applets)

★ `http://www.webmoments.com/java/` (a small collection of special effects applets with easy installation instructions)

★ `http://www.groupboard.com/` (look here for applets that implement chat rooms with white boards)

★ `http://www.free-applets.com/` (a smaller site; nice if you're feeling overwhelmed by too many choices)

★ `http://www.echoecho.com/freeapplets.htm` (a small but select collection; visit the applets tutorial if you're having trouble adding an applet to a Web page)

★ `http://www.jars.com/` (not just applets and not all free, but check out "WWW Tools" under JARS Categories)

★ `http://www.codebrain.com/java/` (beautiful applets, a must-see; check out the Gutenberg applet)

★ `http://java.sun.com/java.sun.com/applets/applets.html` (the birthplace of Java)

★ `http://www.developer.com/directories/pages/dir.java.html` (not just applets; time-consuming to navigate but lots of stuff)

★ `http://www.thefreesite.com/freejava.htm` (a great directory describing lots of free applet sites)

You can search applet archives for applets, or you may discover a nifty applet while surfing the Web. If you see a Web page with a great special effect, check the source code for that page to see whether an applet is responsible. If you can find an applet element, look for the code attribute value inside the applet tag pair. Chances are, it's an applet you can find on the Web if you conduct a keyword search for the applet name at a large general search engine (`Google.com` is a good one to try).

◎◎ Workhorse Applets

It is a rare Web page that never needs to be updated. If your page will need to be updated regularly, you can design it as a **data-driven** page, or more properly, a data-driven display within a Web page. Applets can be especially useful in these situations because you can design an applet to accept data entries that are independent of the applet.

As you learned in the preceding section, you can design applets to accept an entire file as a param value or a single data item such as a hexadecimal color code. This lets you design an applet that receives data from its param values—either directly in the param values themselves or from data files specified in the param values. When you use a parameter for a separate data file that stores text for a Web page display, your Web page is data-driven. For example, consider the problem of maintaining a Web page of announcements that require frequent updates. One approach is to update the underlying HTML file directly. A much cleaner design uses a **text-driven** display: The display engine remains the same and requires no modification. Only the text driving the display is updated.

If you would like to experiment with a text-driven display applet, look at the Gutenberg applet at `CodeBrain.com`—it's amazing.

Data-driven displays are not limited to text. You can find data-driven applets for charts, graphs, and multimedia displays as well. You can use applets to set up slide shows for any number of graphics files, and you can install interactive applets that accept data from the user for user-controlled data-driven displays (for example, a body fat calculator or a movie finder) if you have the right data files to support one. Once you become comfortable with applet installations, you'll be able to bring your Web pages to a whole new level of sophistication.

High-powered applets are not restricted to data-driven displays; some applets add whole new categories of user capabilities to your Web page. For example, you can add a chat room to a Web page. Figure 5.9 shows a nice chat room applet that can be found at `http://www.groupboard.com/`.

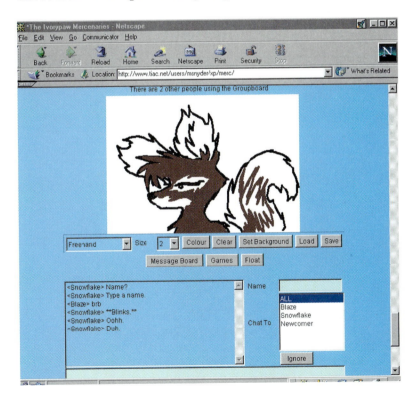

Figure 5.9 A Chat Room with a White Board

This free customizable applet supports a chat room that can hold as many as five people, along with a shared white board. Participants can draw on the white board, and their drawings are broadcast to the other participants in real time.

Programmers are always posting new applets on the Web, and you might even be able to convince someone to write an applet just for you; computer science students sometimes like to try out their newly buff programming muscles on other people's problems just for the experience. And if you like what you can do with other people's applets, you might decide to learn Java so that you can write your own.

The sky's the limit when you can write your own, but don't underestimate what you can do without programming. Applets give the nonprogrammer much of the freedom and creativity that used to require programming expertise or a development budget flush enough to buy it. It's no longer possible to look at a Web page and ascertain the technical expertise of the person who wrote it. Thanks to Java applets and the generosity of the people who distribute their applets for free, some highly sophisticated pages can now be pulled together by nontechnical folks. All you have to do is read and honor the licensing agreements for the applets that you want to use.

☆ Summary

▶ A JavaScript script is a small computer program that's downloaded with a Web page and executed by a JavaScript-enabled browser on the client's host. An applet is a small Java program that's downloaded with a Web page and executed by a Java-enabled browser on the client's host. You don't need to know how to program to install an applet or a script on your Web page.

▶ You can use JavaScript for all sorts of behind-the-scenes Web functionality, including cookie blockers.

▶ A JavaScript script can control the response of your Web page to viewers' mouse movements.

▶ It's easy to use Java applets for special effects such as adding falling snow to a winter scene.

▶ You can add a Java applet to control data-driven displays and other sophisticated Web page functionality.

☆ Online References

HtmlGEAR: free scripts customized by the Web server
http://htmlgear.lycos.com/

HTML Goodies: authoring tools for customizable scripts
http://htmlgoodies.earthweb.com/

JavaScript Search: a source for cut-and-paste scripts
http://www.javascriptsearch.com

JavaScript tutorials
http://webdesign.about.com/msubjscriptinfo.htm

Step by Step Java Tutorial: learn how to write your own Java applets
http://javaboutique.internet.com/tutorials/Step/

☆ Review Questions

1. How are JavaScript scripts inserted into an HTML file? What is a `.js` file?

2. List 10 mouse events that are recognized by JavaScript.

3. Explain how much testing is (ideally) required when you add a new script to a Web page. How do professional programmers deal with the legacy of the "browser wars" when they use JavaScript?

117

4. Which Web page enhancement is more prone to browser compatibility problems—a JavaScript program or an applet? Explain your answer.

5. Can an applet or a script spread computer viruses? Can an applet or a script pass information back to a Web server? What is a malicious script?

6. Compare and contrast JavaScript with Java applets. Describe one way that they are similar and three ways that they are different.

7. How are applets inserted into an HTML file? What do you get when you download an applet from the Net?

8. Why are applets generally easier to install than scripts? How is the customization process different for applets and scripts?

9. What is a data-driven applet? When should you think about adding a data-driven applet to your Web page?

10. Where should you look for installation instructions when you download a JavaScript script? A Java applet?

☆ Hands-On Exercises

1. Visit `http://www.webmoments.com/java/` and find a special-effects applet that you like. Download it, and install it using an image of your own if needed. Did you experience any difficulties with the download or installation of the applet? Describe any problems you encountered. How long did it take to complete a successful installation after you downloaded the applet?

2. Find your own pie chart applet or download the one at `http://home.att.net/~eugenia_kuznetsova/java/piechart/` and customize it for a Web page display. Pick a data set that interests you, or just make one up. How much time did it take you from start to finish? Discuss your experience with the applet. Did you find it easy or difficult to create the display you wanted? Would it be difficult to update this display regularly? Could anybody do it with a little instruction?

3. Download the free demo version of the Gutenberg applet from `http://codebrain.com`. Unpack the download archive and view the applet by opening `0_demo.html`. Then open the file `0_script.txt` with a text editor to see the text file that drives the display. Using this file as a model, see if you can create a text display of your own. To see all of Gutenberg's features (as well as answer the remaining question in this exercise), consult `DOCUMENTATION.txt`. Is the data file for the Gutenberg applet formatted in HTML? Does this applet automatically wrap text from one line to another? What command will make the display pause for one second at the end of a page? How is the `MOUSEOVERSPEED` feature used? How many type fonts and type styles are supported? What is `CLICKMODE`?

4. Go to `http://home.netvigator.com/~freya/ws/js/`
`TypingBanner/TypingBanner.html` to see a script that types messages
in a text box like a ticker tape display. Download the Typing Banner zip file
at the bottom of the page. Configure a Web page to include the typing banner as instructed. This script is stored in a `.js` file instead of an HTML file.
Open `libTypingBanner.js` with a text editor, find where the banner
messages are entered, and replace the default messages with your own messages. The sample configuration cycles through five different messages.
Explain what you would do to make it cycle through six messages instead of
five. ***Note:*** This script may not work with Internet Explorer. If you are using
IE and the display is not working, search a script archive for a similar script
that works with IE (use the keyword "banner").

5. Take two images with the same dimensions and create a Web page with a
mouseover to swap the images when the user passes the mouse over them.
You can adapt the mouseover script described in this chapter to accomplish
this.

CHAPTER SIX

OPEN SOURCE SOFTWARE

No book on freeware and shareware would be complete without an explanation of open source software. Open source software is a growing social movement, a successful—if counterintuitive—business model, and an intriguing bid by computer programmers to control their enterprise for the good of the software. It begins with the observation that software development is not like product development in a traditional manufacturing business. Programmers understand this better than anyone else, and they devised the open source software model in an effort to produce superior software products. The open source movement is thoroughly idealistic as well as pragmatically grounded in real-world experience. Anyone who has encountered the "blue screen of death" on a Windows machine or lived with a Mac that crashes more than it should will want to know about this fascinating world. No one who relies on a computer has to settle for inferior software.

◎◎ Chapter Objectives

⭐ To explore the concept of open source software and its origins

⭐ To examine some common misunderstandings about open source software

⭐ To find out why major commercial software companies are successfully adopting the open source business model

⭐ To look at the implications of open source software for nonprogrammers

◎◎ The Origins of Open Source Software

The concept of open source software was devised in the 1970s by computer programmers for computer programmers. Since then, the open source software movement has expanded to Fortune 500 companies and casual computer users.

To understand the original concept, you must go back to the roots of the open source movement within the programming community. In Chapter One you learned that universities and government-sponsored research projects shaped the ancestral programming community and established respected traditions for shared computer programs. This chapter looks at the psyche of computer programmers to complete a picture that sets the stage for open source software. We start with a look at the discipline of computer programming and the people who are drawn to it.

Computer programming is mentally demanding, labor-intensive work characterized by long hours, creative problem solving, and shifting skill sets that are typically self-taught. Fast-track programmers are usually young adults who have no family responsibilities, work 60 or more hours a week, and consume large amounts of caffeine. In the 1970s and 1980s, the vast majority of programmers were male. That's changing now, but males still predominate. People who are attracted to the profession often find it hard to imagine any other calling.

Most professional programmers hold an undergraduate degree in computer science, know their way around the Internet, and expect to change jobs whenever big projects are terminated and new opportunities arise. Highly competent programmers are self-directed individuals who take pride in their work and their ability to stay on top of a game that requires ongoing continuing education. They look to the Internet and other programmers to identify new developments and trends worth knowing about. Programmers respect other programmers for their technical competence more than their social or economic status, and they do not tolerate incompetence gracefully. Access to new technologies and powerful computing equipment is an important job perk that can rival salary considerations. Young programmers can expect to command generous salaries and benefits, making it possible for them to focus on other aspects of job offers such as technological perks, geographical preferences, or child care availability, among others. Stock options were a standard perk at small start-up companies before the dot-com bubble burst. It's less of a seller's market for programmers these days, but good programmers will always be able to find good jobs.

Computer programmers are, as a whole, a hard-working bunch who take pleasure in tough assignments and challenging projects. They do much of their professional development work at home on their own time and routinely put in long hours if extra time is needed to keep a project on course. Seasoned computer programmers may feel more loyalty to a favorite programming language than to their current employer, but most of them derive professional satisfaction from the quality of their work, so employers generally benefit from the programmers' ethos. Indeed, it can be difficult to motivate a programmer with salary raises or even the threat of a layoff if a work assignment is not intrinsically satisfying in its own right. As a rule, computer programmers enjoy being challenged.

Some of the most valuable software contributions made by lone programmers weren't conceived as corporate projects or part of a formal job description. Rather, they were the result of "developer's itch." Programmers who see how a specific software tool could ease the daily routine or streamline a project may experience this itch. A programmer motivated by the itch experiences the strongest possible work perk: an opportunity to write code that stirs the soul. This is when the creative juices flow most freely and personal satisfaction is at its highest. In fact, it can be difficult to pull a programmer away from a beloved programming problem (as many a neglected spouse will readily attest), whether or not it's part of the job. It's plausible that programmers who never experience the itch enjoy far less job satisfaction than those who are periodically obsessed with pet projects.

In a profession where job satisfaction depends on the quality of one's work as much as one's paycheck, workers work to please themselves at least as much as they work to please the boss. Similarly, social status is less a matter of corporate kudos and more a question of hard-won respect from one's peers (who may very well work for other companies). And how does a programmer win recognition for excellence in programming? There's only one way: by sharing code with other programmers.

> ☆ **TIP**   **Source Code Files, Executable Files, and Proprietary Programs**
>
> Computer programs can be distributed as executable files or source code files. An executable file can be launched and run but cannot be read and understood by humans. To understand the code behind an executable file, you must examine the source code, which is written in programming languages such as Java or Visual Basic. These files can be read and modified by anyone who knows the programming language. When I talk about "sharing code" or "posting programs" in this chapter, I'm talking about shared source code, not shared executables. Proprietary software is distributed as executables only. No one can modify or build on code that is available only in executable files.

Shared software has always been freely distributed over the Internet from the early days of ARPA-sponsored research projects. Programmers who post their code on the Internet can reap the praises of their peers (or at least some candid feedback), whereas programmers who are bound by proprietary software agreements must hide their creations within a corporate castle, toiling in professional obscurity and social isolation. If you've worked on a program for months or years, it's gratifying to post it on the Net. It's not enough to distribute executable files: To evaluate a program, other programmers need to see its source code. The distribution of source code alongside an executable program file is the hallmark of open source software. **Open source** means openly available source code.

Social recognition is only one reason—and perhaps not even the most compelling reason—programmers share their source code with the world. Programmers who find source code on the Net do not simply read and evaluate it. When the code is useful, they often find ways to improve it, extend it, and rework it in new directions. People who modify open source software can send their contributions to the original author, and a new version of the software can be distributed with the improvement in place. Software generally benefits from this public scrutiny and modification. When source code is freely subjected to the public scrutiny of independent-minded programmers all over the world, favorable public opinion propels the software into the spotlight, and unfavorable evaluations lay the software to rest in a quiet corner of the software world where few visitors venture.

⭐ **SHORTCUT**   **Open Source Software Explained**

For a succinct explanation of open source software, visit `http://www.opensource.org`. Among other things, you'll find this statement: "The basic idea behind open source is very simple. When programmers on the Internet can read, redistribute, and modify the source for a piece of software, it evolves. People improve it, people adapt it, people fix bugs. And this can happen at a speed that, if one is used to the slow pace of conventional software development, seems astonishing. We in the open-source community have learned that this rapid evolutionary process produces better software than the traditional closed model, in which only a very few programmers can see source and everybody else must blindly use an opaque block of bits."

The open source software movement is all about protecting the evolutionary process that results when programmers who openly post their source code for widespread public scrutiny, possible code modifications, and redistribution. Open source software is generally protected by one key idea:

> Anyone can download open source software, use that software, and even modify it, as long as all redistributions of the software are also open source distributions: No one can claim proprietary rights to either the original software or any modified versions of the original software.

A typical open source software license is more detailed than this (see Exercise 1 at the end of this chapter), but that's the core idea.

The open source theme has many variations. The Open Source Initiative specifies a set of conditions that a software license must meet in order to be OSI-certified. Richard M. Stallman developed the **GNU General Public License (GPL)**, an older license for open source software. The **lesser GPL (LGPL)** is a modified, and somewhat less strict, version of the original GPL. BSD-UNIX, a version of UNIX developed at the University of California, Berkeley, was first developed in 1977, making BSD-UNIX the first open source operating system. In 1984, however, the federal government granted AT&T the right to enter the computer business, and AT&T immediately reclaimed UNIX as a proprietary product.

Although Stallman has never endorsed the "open source" nomenclature—he believes it's important to use the term *free* software to emphasize the key concept of freedom in software development—he is a prominent advocate and spokesman for the open source software movement. Stallman founded the Free Software Foundation (FSF) in 1985, partly in response to AT&T's increasingly expensive commercialization of UNIX. His goal was to create a free operating system (really a free version of UNIX). Stallman and his FSF staff created and refined many popular software tools for UNIX (including GNU Emacs and the GNU C compiler).

☆**TIP**   **Free Speech Versus Free Beer**

When Richard Stallman talks about free software, he is not talking about software that costs nothing (in the same way we talk about "free beer"); rather, he is talking about software that has been liberated from proprietary constraints (in the same way we talk about "free speech"). Under the General Public License, GPL software can be distributed free of charge, or it can be distributed for a fee. Either way, Stallman calls it free software. When Stallman distributes his own GPL software, his licensing fees are voluntary. Everyone is welcome to download and use Stallman's software at no charge. If the software proves to be useful, Stallman trusts people to pay for it on a voluntary basis. He believes people will pay, in good conscience, for things that they use and value.

In 1991, Linus Torvalds, a Finnish computer science student, began work on a key component for a free version of UNIX, using his own "release early, release often" approach to software development. If a release contained bugs, Torvalds relied on an army of enthusiastic volunteers to find and fix them. The Linux operating system (see Figure 6.1) was first released in 1992, setting the stage for increased interest in open source software in the late 1990s.

Figure 6.1 Linux, a Popular Open Source Alternative to Windows

In 1997, Eric S. Raymond, another leader in the open source movement, wrote an influential essay, "The Cathedral and the Bazaar," which sparked wider interest in open source software. The following year, Netscape released the source code for its Web browser, drawing even more attention to the movement and arousing widespread interest in the commercial sector.

The Linux operating system has spawned commercial Linux releases and gained widespread acceptance as a viable software platform in business environments, with both Dell and IBM offering it preinstalled on recent computer models. Open source software is slowly but surely making the shift from computer professionals to mainstream computer users.

Open Source Myths and Misunderstandings

This section explores some erroneous assumptions and common misunderstandings about open source software.

Open Source Software Can't Be Commercial

Open source software licenses do not prohibit licensing fees. Anyone who believes that a program has potential as a commercial product can redistribute it as open source software and charge people for it. The only catch is that someone else could redistribute exactly the same software for free. Commercial software is usually distributed with strict prohibitions against unauthorized redistributions. With so many commercial software firms losing significant revenues to software pirates, how can a company turn a profit by charging for open source software? Why would users pay for something they can get for free?

> ☆ **TIP** Anyone can add value to an open source software distribution. If the total package is commercially viable, you've got a commercial product.

As strange as it may seem, many companies are turning a profit by selling open source software. All the commercial distributions of Linux (such as Red Hat Linux) impose fee-based licensing agreements on Linux, which can be downloaded free from the Net. Perhaps some users don't know it's available for free, but most users are happy to pay for a "value-added" version. How do companies add value? They might, for example, include superior software documentation or offer superior customer support.

It Can't Be Any Good Because It's Free

Anyone growing up in a capitalist society is inclined to confuse the price of a commodity with its value. How many times have you heard the warning "You get what you pay for"?

In reality, though, a price/value correlation is solid for some products but less certain for others. When it comes to software, prices do not necessarily predict quality. Open source software is generally subjected to a much more rigorous and thorough review process than proprietary software undergoes. The reviewers are independent developers, and the open source license encourages rapid software evolution. As a result, successful adaptations receive widespread support, and unsuccessful ones are left by the wayside. Interestingly, the open source review process is especially effective on very large software programs, where oddball bugs may be difficult to discover during routine testing.

To Get Good Customer Support You Must Pay for It

Again, conventional wisdom tends to fall down in the face of open source software. Consider *InfoWorld's* Best Technical Support Award. This award is usually given to the software vendor who receives the most votes from *InfoWorld* readers. Although software support might not be one of the computer industry's shining achievements, at least a few companies always manage to do it well, and their grateful users speak out by making nominations and casting votes for the *InfoWorld* award.

In 1997, the Best Technical Support Award went to the Linux user community. This open source operating system is usually distributed without commercial technical support. Users who have questions and problems must rely on the kindness of strangers in newsgroups and message boards. This altruistic system of customer support can work quite well, as the award attests. In the case of Linux, free support from fellow users is apparently as good as, if not better than, commercial help desk support.

Big Companies Can't Afford to Experiment with Open Source Software

Why would a successful company want to cut corners on software if it can afford the best? Again, this question confuses price with value. Paying top dollar for a piece of software does not necessarily mean you're getting the best software available. And anyone who's ever gone through the procurement procedure at a large company knows that nothing happens very fast when money changes hands via corporate channels. Forms must be filled out, approved by middle management, and processed by paper pushers. Programmers are generally under pressure to produce fast results, and even a 24-hour delay is unthinkable for a project that's already behind schedule (note that it is notoriously difficult to keep software projects on schedule even under optimal circumstances).

From a programmer's perspective, a software download from the Internet (freeware, shareware, or open source) is the best way to obtain software whenever you need something you don't want to write yourself. Software available on the Net can be put to work right away and then paid for after its suitability has been established. Immediate software availability without paperwork and executive approval helps programmers hit milestones on time, and it encourages experimentation with multiple solutions—something that's often crucial for a project's success.

Software experimentation entails time-consuming trials, which presumably could be avoided with the right magic bullet. Why should anyone experiment with in-house software if the solution is available commercially?

> ☆ **WARNING** Detailed software documentation does not always tell programmers everything they need to know about an unfamiliar software product. There is no substitute for a hands-on trial run, where a new software product is run in conjunction with other software components and evaluated in a context that may never have been anticipated by the product's original programmers.

Programmers are usually happy to use existing software whenever possible, but finding workable software solutions is no small accomplishment.

Reliable, usable software is not necessarily the most expensive product with the glossiest brochures and the most polished sales personnel. Instead, it may be a little-known freeware, shareware, or open source product. There is no way of knowing where the best solution is without experimentation and evaluation. If the software under consideration is open source software, you can start with something that may be 95% of the solution and make crucial adjustments to cover the other 5%. Any project manager who thinks the team can't afford to experiment with different software solutions has no firsthand experience with software development.

◎◎ Open Source Success Stories

Many key software components responsible for the operation of the Internet are open source software programs. Given the crucial nature of these components, it's difficult to see how the Internet could have evolved without the developmental process associated with open source software. It was big news when Netscape announced in 1998 that it would distribute its flagship product, Netscape Communicator, as open source software. But open source software had been working quietly behind the scenes of the Internet long before 1998. Here are some examples.

Sendmail

Each time you send an e-mail message, chances are your e-mail relies on a program called Sendmail. Sendmail was developed by Eric Allman in 1981 at UC Berkeley to enable mail deliveries across different computer networks, a key requirement for seamless global communications. Sendmail was initially distributed with BSD-UNIX, under the Berkeley Systems Distribution license (an open source distribution) and remains open source to this day.

Perl

Motivated by a desire to produce something useful, Larry Wall released the first version of the Perl programming language in 1987. Wall's concern for flexible utility led him to an open distribution. Originally conceived as a language for system administrators, Perl has become the premier programming language for Web programmers. Perl works behind the scenes at all the big (as well as the lesser) e-commerce sites—from Amazon.com to Yahoo!

Apache

Most computer users understand how important it is to have a Web browser, but browsers would be useless without Web servers. A **Web server** is a computer that distributes Web pages on demand, something that requires special server software. Brian Behlendorf initiated an open source Web server project in 1995, and it quickly became the most widely used software of its type. Behlendorf's philosophy was to "share the responsibility for the code very widely amongst people that you trust, and we'll do more than any one person can do." In 1998, IBM adopted Apache as the Web server for its WebSphere product line. The decision by IBM to replace its own in-house Web server with the open source Apache server created considerable interest in open source software as a respectable option for major corporations.

Jikes

IBM's own contribution to open source software was a Java compiler, Jikes, first released in 1998 (see Figure 6.2). The open source license used for Jikes was generalized into the IBM Public License in June 1999. The Jikes compiler is not used as extensively as the Java compiler distributed by Sun Microsystems, but IBM's adaptation of the open source model for one of its own software products showed how compelling the open source idea had become, even within the company's famously conservative culture.

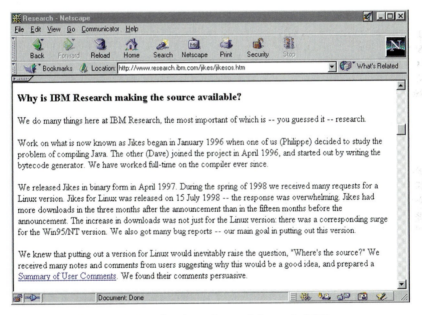

Figure 6.2 IBM Began to Develop Open Source Software in 1998

Linux

Linux, an open source version of the UNIX operating system, is arguably the most ambitious open source software effort to date. Under development since 1991, Linux began as the pet project of Linus Torvalds. In 1999, computer manufacturer Hewlett-Packard began distributing Linux preinstalled on HP computers. More importantly, HP announced around-the-clock technical support for Linux and all HP Linux-based applications. In short order, hardware vendors Dell, IBM, Compaq, SGI, and Gateway announced their support for Linux. With support from the major hardware vendors, Linux was positioned to challenge Microsoft's NT/2000 platform, something no traditional software house could do. The story of Linux and its impact on commercial computing can be found in *Rebel Code: Inside Linux and the Open Source Revolution*, by Glyn Moody (Perseus Publishing, 2001).

Open Source Software and You

Open source software is compelling as a software development strategy. But if you're not a computer programmer, what does it mean to you? Although Linux and open source Linux applications are making steady inroads in corporate environments and on college campuses, most open source software is best handled by software professionals. Open source software can be difficult to install and difficult to use. Efforts to outfit Linux with a graphical user interface (to make it look more like Windows or a Macintosh desktop) are helping to broaden its appeal, but most open source software was never designed as application software for general users. Most users will never need to install Apache software on a Web server or write their own behind-the-scene scripts in Perl. So the open source software movement is not likely to revolutionize the lives of casual computer users any time soon.

However, open source software is challenging the very concept of proprietary software and the commercial business model that drives Microsoft and almost every other commercial software company. The standard commercial software model, epitomized by Microsoft, relies on limited access to executable software files through stringent licensing agreements and proprietary restrictions on source code files. All proprietary code is developed in-house and often is flawed despite considerable effort to crank out a robust and reliable product. Corporate profits on popular software titles are seriously undermined by software piracy, and software manufacturers look to the law to enforce licensing agreements.

In the open source software model, in contrast, piracy is not a problem, and extensive software testing (at no cost) is the norm. But consider what happens when a company decides to distribute open source software commercially. Companies who sell open source software are really selling customer support (few companies are likely to adopt Richard Stallman's voluntary payment model). It follows that when open source software goes mainstream, the big winner is the consumer.

Bill Gates was quick to condemn practices associated with software piracy at the dawn of Microsoft's software empire, and he understands the more profound threat that Linux poses to Microsoft's operating system monopoly today. (At the time of this writing, an appeals court has upheld charges against Microsoft for monopolistic practices with respect to Microsoft's marketing of Windows.) Internal Microsoft documents written in 1998 (see Exercise 5) explain how futile it is for Microsoft to fight the open source software threat based on the merit of its product line alone. There is little one can do to halt a competitor that can undercut any price with software that is as good or better than yours.

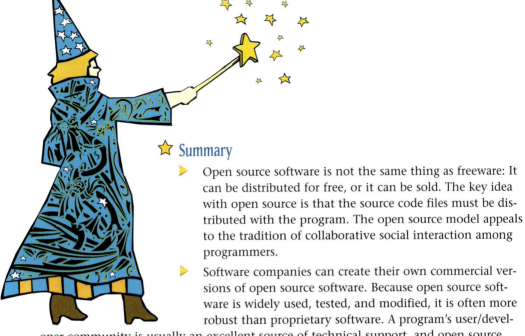

⭐ Summary

- ▶ Open source software is not the same thing as freeware: It can be distributed for free, or it can be sold. The key idea with open source is that the source code files must be distributed with the program. The open source model appeals to the tradition of collaborative social interaction among programmers.

- ▶ Software companies can create their own commercial versions of open source software. Because open source software is widely used, tested, and modified, it is often more robust than proprietary software. A program's user/developer community is usually an excellent source of technical support, and open source software is used in a wide variety of commercial enterprises.

- ▶ Numerous open source programs, including Linux, Sendmail, and Apache, attest to the success of the open source model of software development.

- ▶ Even nonprogrammers have a stake in the open source model because it has the potential to compete with widely used proprietary software, including Windows.

⭐ Online References

Open Source Initiative
http://www.opensource.org

Bruce Perens explains open source software
http://www.oreilly.com/catalog/opensources/book/perens.html

The Story of the Free Software Project
http://www.gnu.org/philosophy/why-free.html

The Cathedral and the Bazaar
http://www.tuxedo.org/~esr/writings/cathedral-bazaar/

Open Source Schools (Educators support open source resources)
http://members.iteachnet.org/opensourceschools/links.php

Simple End User Linux
http://www.seul.org/

Microsoft Cracks Down on Piracy in the Public Schools
http://www.salon.com/tech/feature/2001/07/10/microsoft_school/index.html

☆ Review Questions

1. Explain the core idea behind open source software.

2. What event triggered the creation of the Free Software Foundation? When was the FSF founded?

3. When was Linux first released?

4. What popular Web browser was released as open source software after the publication of "The Cathedral and the Bazaar"? When did this take place?

5. What does Richard Stallman mean when he talks about "free" software?

6. Suppose you rely on open source software and you run into a problem that you can't handle. Where can you go for help?

7. How can it make sense for a software company to sell a product that can be obtained for free? Give an example of such a company.

8. Name three pieces of open source software that help make the Internet operational. Describe what they do.

9. What software won *InfoWorld*'s Best Technical Support Award for 1997? Who picks the recipients of this award? Explain why the 1997 award was surprising.

10. What did IBM do in 1998 that enhanced the status of open source software?

☆ Hands-On Exercises

1. Look up the definition of open source software at `http://www.opensource.org/docs/definition_plain.html` and name the nine main requirements of an open source software license.

2. Visit `http://www.tuxedo.org/~esr/writings/cathedral-bazaar/` to read Eric S. Raymond's original essay "The Cathedral and the Bazaar." Explain the symbolism behind the cathedral and the bazaar: What does the cathedral represent? What does the bazaar represent?

3. A detailed definition of open source software is presented at `http://www.perens.com/OSD.html`. Review this document and answer the following questions. How is open source software different from software in the public domain? Can the same program be distributed under an open source license and also under a commercial license? If anyone can modify and redistribute open source software, how can users know which version they're getting? Can someone make a trivial modification to an open source program and then market the slightly modified program under a commercial license?

4. Go out on the Net and find out what UCITA is. Then read "Why We Must Fight UCITA" by Richard Stallman at `http://www.gnu.org/ philosophy/ucita.html`. Explain briefly what UCITA is and why it is a threat to the open source software movement.

5. Peruse the "Halloween documents" at `http://www.opensource.org/ halloween/` to find out how Microsoft engineers were talking about open source software in general and Linux in particular in 1998. Then answer the following questions. When were the Halloween documents written? Who published the Halloween documents, and how were they obtained? What two claims did Microsoft publicly advance to counter public interest in Linux? (**Hint:** See Halloween V for an interview with Microsoft spokesperson Ed Muth.) What does FUD mean, and what companies are in a position to exploit it?

APPENDIX A: ONLINE RESOURCES

Chapter One (Software on the Internet)

Internet History
http://www.isoc.org/internet/history/

Freeware: The Heart and Soul of the Internet
http://www.oreilly.com/news/freeware_0398.html

The History of Shareware and PsL
http://www.pslweb.com/history.htm

Information Wants to Be Free
http://www.anu.edu.au/people/Roger.Clarke/II/IWtbF.html

Understanding Software Licenses
http://allbusiness.com/cmt/information/general.
jsp?fname=201

Chapter Two (Downloading and Installing Software)

Downloading Software from the Internet: PC TechPaper Tutorial for Beginners
http://www.siliconguide.com/internet/download/download.
shtml

Downloading Software for the Mac
http://cybered.umassd.edu/public/CyberEdHelp/tutorial/
downMAC.html

Downloading Software and Files: It's Easier Than You Think
http://www.rmlibrary.com/news/news03.htm

ZDNet Help and How-To: How To Protect against Computer Viruses
http://www.zdnet.com/zdhelp/stories/main/
0,5594,2248291,00.html

An Overview of Computer Viruses and Antivirus Software
http://www.hicom.net/~oedipus/virus32.html

Preventing Possible Web Intrusions: Learn To Disable ActiveX, Java,
and JavaScript
http://www.smartcomputing.com/editorial/article.asp?
article=articles%2Farchive%2Fg0804%2F37g04%2F37g04%2Easp

◎◎ Chapter Three (Customizing Your Online Experience)

Help! Plug-Ins
http://www1.sympatico.ca/help/Plugins/

Learn the Net: Plug-Ins
http://www.learnthenet.com/english/html/56plugins.htm

Cookie Central
http://cookiecentral.com/

Junkbusters
http://www.junkbusters.com/

◎◎ Chapter Four (Essential Tools for Web Page Authors)

Arachnophilia
http://www.arachnoid.com/arachnophilia/

ButtonMaker 2.3.1
http://www.mlanier.f2s.com/downloads.php

Dr. Bill's Image Converter and Map Generator
http://www-unix.oit.umass.edu/~verts/software/
software.html#IMAGEMAP

GraphicConverter
http://lemkesoft.com/us_gcabout.html

HTML Editors and Associated Tools (mostly for Windows)
http://webdevelopersjournal.com/software/html_editors.html

HTML-Kit
http://www.chami.com/

HTML TIDY
http://www.w3.org/People/Raggett/tidy/

ImageForge
http://www.cursorarts.com/ca_imffw.html

IrfanView
http://www.irfanview.com/

SiteSucker
http://members.aol.com/rcranisky/sitesucker.html

Splitz!
http://www.b-zone.de/software/splitz.htm

SynEdit
http://www.mkidesign.com/syneditinfo.html

Top HTML Editors for the Mac (suitable for both beginners and professionals)
http://macworld.zdnet.com/netsmart/features/
editorintro.html

URL Manager
http://www.url-manager.com/

WS_FTP LE/WS_FTP PRO
http://www.ipswitch.com/Purchase/index.html

Xenu's Link Sleuth
http://home.snafu.de/tilman/xenulink.html

◎◎ Chapter Five (Scripts and Applets)

HtmlGEAR: Free scripts customized by the Web server
http://htmlgear.lycos.com/

HTML Goodies: Authoring tools for customizable scripts
http://htmlgoodies.earthweb.com/

JavaScript Search: A source for cut-and-paste scripts
http://www.javascriptsearch.com

JavaScript Tutorials
http://webdesign.about.com/msubjscriptinfo.htm

Step-by-Step Java Tutorial: Learn how to write your own Java applets
http://javaboutique.internet.com/tutorials/Step/

◎◎ Chapter Six (Open Source Software)

Open Source Initiative
http://www.opensource.org

Bruce Perens explains open source software.
http://www.oreilly.com/catalog/opensources/book/perens.html

The Story of the Free Software Project
http://www.gnu.org/philosophy/why-free.html

The Cathedral and the Bazaar
http://www.tuxedo.org/~esr/writings/cathedral-bazaar/

Open Source Schools (Educators support open source resources)
http://members.iteachnet.org/opensourceschools/links.php

Simple End User Linux
http://www.seul.org/

Microsoft Cracks Down on Piracy in the Public Schools
http://www.salon.com/tech/feature/2001/07/10/microsoft_school/index.html

APPENDIX B: FILE TYPES

This appendix is a catalogue of file types commonly found in file archives on the Internet, along with the most popular file utilities needed to handle them. Most file types are platform-specific, so we have grouped them under their associated operating systems: Macintosh, PC, and UNIX. This is not a comprehensive list, but it does cover the files you are most likely to encounter.

Macintosh Files

File Extensions	What Is It?	Some Available Utilities
.bin	MacBinary is a binary format for encoding Mac files so they can be safely stored on non-Mac platforms	MacBinary II+ Stuffit Expander
.sit	a compressed file archive created by Stuffit Deluxe	Unstuffit Deluxe Stuffit Expander
.hqx	Binhex4 is an ASCII format for encoding binary files for text-based communication channels	BinHex DeHQX Stuffit Expander
.sea	a self-extracting archive	none needed
.uue	uuencoding is an ASCII format for encoding binary files for text-based communication channels	UULite UUundo
.dd	a file compressed with DiskDoubler	Disk Doubler Expander
.pdf	a Portable Document Format file	open it with Adobe Acrobat or Adobe Acrobat Reader
.cpt	a compressed file archive created by Compact Pro	Extractor Stuffit Expander

◎◎ PC Files

File Extensions	What Is It?	Some Available Utilities
.zip	a compressed file archive	PKUNZIP UNZIP WinZip WinUnZip
.exe	usually an executable file but can also be a self-extracting archive	none needed
.uue	uuencoding is an ASCII format for encoding binary files for text-based communication channels	uucode xferp wpack
.ps	a printable ASCII Postscript file	just send it to a Postscript printer or Postscript viewer
.pdf	a Portable Document Format file	open it with Adobe Acrobat or Adobe Acrobat Reader
.wp	a WordPerfect file	open it with a Word processor

◎◎ UNIX Files

File Extensions	What Is It?	Some Available Utilities
.gz	a compressed file archive created with gzip	gzip gunzp
.Z	a compressed file	uncompress gzip
.tar	a file archive (not compressed)	tar detar
.uue	uuencoding is an ASCII format for encoding binary files for text-based communication channels	uudecode
.shar	a self-extracting file archive	sh (but you must be in the UNIX Bourne shell)

File Extensions	What Is It?	Some Available Utilities
`.ps`	a printable ASCII Postscript file	just send it to a Postscript printer or Postscript viewer
`.exe`	usually an executable but it can also be a self-extracting archive	none needed
`.tZ` `.tarZ` `.tar.Z`	rename it as `.tar.Z` and handle it in two steps (see above)	(first uncompress it, then untar it)
`.tgz` `.tar.gz`	rename it as `tar.gz` and handle it in two steps (see above)	(first unzip it, then untar it)

APPENDIX C: SOFTWARE RESOURCES

This appendix contains URLs for software examples mentioned in this book. The inclusion of a specific software title on this list does not constitute an endorsement by the author. Always research your software selections as much as possible before you download and install.

AntiVirus Software

McAfee VirusScan
http://www.mcafee.com/
Norton AntiVirus
http://www.norton.com/

Applet Libraries

http://javaboutique.internet.com/ (one of the major sites)

http://freewarejava.com/ (another large site)

http://wsabstract.com/java/ (another large site)

http://www.javapowered.com/ (nice stuff; visit the showcase and check out the newest applets)

http://www.webmoments.com/java/ (a small collection of special effects applets with easy installation instructions)

http://www.groupboard.com/ (look here for applets that implement chat rooms with white boards)

http://www.free-applets.com/ (a smaller site; nice if you're feeling overwhelmed by too many choices)

http://www.echoecho.com/freeapplets.htm (a small but select collection; visit the applets tutorial if you're having trouble adding an applet to a Web page)

http://www.jars.com/ (not just applets and not all free, but check out "WWW Tools" under JARS Categories)

http://www.codebrain.com/java/ (beautiful applets, a must-see; check out the Gutenberg applet)

http://java.sun.com/java.sun.com/applets/applets.html (the birthplace of Java)

`http://www.developer.com/directories/pages/dir.java.html`
(not just applets; time-consuming to navigate, but lots of stuff)

`http://www.thefreesite.com/freejava.htm` (a great directory describing lots of free applet sites)

◎◎ Document Viewers

Adobe Acrobat Reader
`http://www.adobe.com/`

MS Word Viewer
`http://office.microsoft.com/downloads/2000/wd97vwr32.aspx`
(for Windows)

PowerPoint Viewer
`http://office.microsoft.com/downloads/9798/ppview97.aspx`
(for Windows)

`http://www.microsoft.com/mac/download/office98/`
`powerpoint98viewer.asp` (for Macintosh)

◎◎ Download Managers

GetRight (Windows)
`http://www.getright.com/`

Go!Zilla (Windows)
`http://www.gozilla.com/`

Download Deputy (Macintosh)
`http://www.ilesa.com/`

◎◎ File Utilities

WinZip (Windows)
`http://www.winzip.com/tucows/`

ZipCentral (Windows)
`http://zipcentral.iscool.net/`

Stuffit Expander (Macintosh)
`http://www.stuffit.com/expander/macindex.html`

◎◎ Graphics Programs

IrfanView
`http://www.irfanview.com/`

ImageForge
`http://www.cursorarts.com/ca_imffw.html`

GraphicConverter
`http://lemkesoft.com/us_gcabout.html`

◉◉ JavaScript Libraries

`http://JavaScript.internet.com/` (a good site for beginners)

`http://www.24fun.ch/`

`http://www.developer.com/downloads/code/JavaScripts.html`

`http://www.essex1.com/people/timothy/js-index.htm` (a good site for beginners)

`http://www.exeat.com/`

`http://www.freecode.com/`

`http://www.geocities.com/SiliconValley/7116/`

`http://www.infohiway.com/JavaScript/indexf.htm`

`http://www.JavaScripts.com/`

`http://www.JavaScriptsearch.com/`

`http://www.js-planet.com/`

`http://www.scripts.com/JavaScript/`

`http://www.thefreesite.com/freejava.htm`

`http://www.webmonkey.com/`

`http://www.wsabstract.com/` (a good site for beginners)

◉◉ Miscellaneous Software

FreeMem Professional
`http://www.meikel.com/en/products/freemem/`

Comet Cursor
`http://www.cometsystems.com/`

ZoneAlarm
`http://www.zonelabs.com/`

EyeDropper
`http://eyedropper.inetia.com/HTML/eng/default.asp`

MailTo-Encrypter
`http://pluto.spaceports.com/~mobysw/en/mailto-encrypter.html`

Copernic
`http://www.copernic.com/`

◎◎ Multimedia Players

QuickTime
http://www.apple.com/quicktime/

RealPlayer
http://www.real.com/

Shockwave
http://sdc.shockwave.com/shockwave/

Windows Media Player
http://windowsmedia.microsoft.com/download/download.asp

◎◎ Plug-In Libraries

★ Official Netscape Plug-In Directory: http://home.netscape.com/
  plugins/index.html

★ Plug-In Plaza: http://browserwatch.internet.com/plug-in.
  html

★ ZDNet > Help & How-To > Internet > Plug-Ins:
  http://www.zdnet.com/zdhelp/filters/subfilter/
  0,7212,6003243,00.html

◎◎ Software Clearinghouses

Tucows
http://www.tucows.com

DOWNLOAD.COM
http://download.cnet.com

ZDNet Downloads
http://www.zdnet.com/downloads/

Dave Central Software Archive
http://www.davecentral.com

MACDOWNLOAD.COM
http://www.zdnet.com/mac/download.html

SHAREWARE.COM
http://shareware.cnet.com/

More Software Archives (for Windows):

★ http://www.webattack.com/

★ http://www.getyoursfree.com/

★ http://www.mysharewarepage.com/webtools.htm

★ http://www.completelyfreesoftware.com/
★ http://www.nonags.com/
★ http://www.Slaughterhouse.com/pick.html
★ http://www.completelyfreesoftware.com/index_all.html
★ http://www.32bit.com/
★ http://www.freewareweb.com/
★ http://www.thefreesite.com/
★ http://www.rocketdownload.com
★ http://www.hotfiles.com/
★ http://www.winmag.com
★ http://softsite.com/
★ http://happypuppy.com/
★ http://newapps.internet.com/categories.html
★ http://www.galttech.com/sharware.shtml
★ http://cws.internet.com/
★ http://www.netigen.com/freeware.html

More Software Archives (for Macintosh):

★ http://www.ultimatemac.com.
★ http://maccentral.macworld.com/
★ http://www.macresource.com/mrp/software.shtml
★ http://www.macorchard.com/
★ http://www.chezmark.com/
★ http://www.macupdate.com/
★ http://hyperarchive.lcs.mit.edu/HyperArchive/
★ http://asu.info.apple.com/
★ http://www.versiontracker.com/
★ http://www.tidbits.com/iskm/iskm-soft.html
★ http://Macs.Bon.Net/MacFreeware_Os_1024x768.html

◉◉ Software Reviews

All Operating Systems:

★ The Cool Tool Network (http://www.cooltool.com/search.cgi)
★ ZDNet Reviews (http://www.zdnet.com/products/)

Windows:

★ Stroud's CWSA Apps (`http://cws.internet.com/`)

★ Win Planet Reviews (`http://www.winplanet.com/winplanet/subjects/`)

★ Digital Duck (`http://www.digitalduck.com/`)

★ Netigen Web (`http://www.netigen.com/reviews.html`)

★ PCToday.com Supersite (`http://www.pctoday.com/mini/smartcomputing/editorial/reviews.asp?rid=396&guid=wlvapo30`)

★ PCWORLD.COM Reviews (`http://www.pcworld.com/top400/0,1375,software,00.html`)

Macintosh:

★ MacReview Zone (`http://www.macreviewzone.com/`)

★ MacDirectory (`http://www.pacifeeder.com/macintosh/software.htm`)

★ Macs Only (`http://www.macsonly.com/`)

★ MacHome Journal Online Reviews (`http://database.machome.com/Reviews/reviews.lasso`)

◎◎ Tools for Web Page Authors

Arachnophilia
`http://www.arachnoid.com/arachnophilia/`

ButtonMaker 2.3.1
`http://www.mlanier.f2s.com/downloads.php`

Dr. Bill's Image Converter and Map Generator
`http://www-unix.oit.umass.edu/~verts/software/software.html#IMAGEMAP`

HTML Editors and Associated Tools (mostly for Windows)
`http://webdevelopersjournal.com/software/html_editors.html`

HTML-Kit
`http://www.chami.com/`

HTML TIDY
`http://www.w3.org/People/Raggett/tidy/`

SiteSucker
`http://members.aol.com/rcranisky/sitesucker.html`

Splitz!
`http://www.b-zone.de/software/splitz.htm`

SynEdit
http://www.mkidesign.com/syneditinfo.html

WS_FTP LE/WS_FTP PRO
http://www.ipswitch.com/Purchase/index.html

Link Sleuth
http://home.snafu.de/tilman/xenulink.html

◎◎ Web Browsers

Internet Explorer
http://www.microsoft.com/windows/ie/default.htm

Netscape Communicator
http://home.netscape.com/

Opera
http://www.opera.com/

◎◎ Web-Related Managers

Cookie Pal
http://www.kburra.com/cpal.html

AdSubtract SE
http://www.adsubtract.com/

Cookie Crusher
http://www.thelimitsoft.com/

MagicCookie Monster
http://download.at/drjsoftware/

Password Prompter
http://www.zdnet.com/pcmag/pctech/content/18/11/
ut1811.001.html

Gator
http://www.gator.com/

URL Manager
http://www.url-manager.com/

APPENDIX D: ANSWERS TO ODD-NUMBERED REVIEW QUESTIONS

◎◎ Chapter One

1. ARPA (Advanced Research Projects Agency), which is part of the Department of Defense, sponsored most of the early research. The work itself was conducted mostly at universities in the United States.

3. Shareware is software that can be used at no charge during a trial examination period. After that, users are required either to pay for the software or to uninstall it.

5. Programmers sometimes work on problems for their own enjoyment. They like to get feedback and suggestions from other programmers, and they know they will get a larger user population if they distribute their program as freeware.

7. A registration key is a string of text that can be typed into a program to "unlock" its full capabilities. Registration keys are given to people who have paid for a piece of software that is freely distributed over the Internet. Only users with registration keys will be able to run the full version of the software.

9. It all depends on the software license. In some cases, the answer will be yes; in other cases, no.

◎◎ Chapter Two

1. Software that runs on one platform will not normally run on other platforms.

3. Running "from its current location" means running it from a temporary location on your computer instead of from files on the hard drive. This is not a good idea because your antivirus software won't have an opportunity to examine the program before you execute it. The only time this option might make sense is if you've downloaded this same software from this same location before, scanned it for viruses, and determined that it's safe to execute. In that case, running from its current location may save you from having to delete unneeded files later.

5. An installer is a program that walks users through the installation of complicated software that would otherwise be difficult to install by hand. Programs are packaged inside installers to make the installation process easy and error-free. An installer is usually run only once, but some people like to save installers in case they ever need to reinstall or move the software to a new computer.

7. It's safe for a browser to open a data file (e.g., an audio file or an animation file) with an appropriate viewer. But it's dangerous for a browser to open an executable file because it might contain a computer virus.

9. Exit all other running applications.

◎◎ Chapter Three

1. A plug-in is an application that displays files inside the browser's window, as if it were part of the browser. An add-on is an application that can be launched by clicking on a browser icon, but the application runs in its own window, separate from the browser.

3. (a) add-on (b) plug-in (c) plug-in (d) plug-in (e) add-on

5. You have to disable cookies, either selectively or altogether. Turning off all the graphics won't do it.

7. Encrypt it instead of saving it in an unprotected text file. PassProm is one application where sensitive information, such as credit card numbers, can be encrypted and password-protected.

9. A password manager makes it easy to use unique userids and passwords for all the Web sites that require them. Using different userids and passwords is important because if one is compromised, the others are still secure. You can also use a password manager to store other sensitive information, such as credit card numbers, in a safe (encrypted) format that is password-protected.

◎◎ Chapter Four

1. Many FTP client can (1) queue multiple files for large uploading or downloading jobs, (2) display local and remote directories simultaneously, (3) schedule file transfers at convenient times, and (4) resume an interrupted file transfer.

3. TIDY is especially useful when you've inherited poorly written HTML from someone else, or when you have to deal with HTML that was generated by an HTML converter that doesn't generate good HTML.

5. Web browsers are normally configured to display only GIF and JPG files (although Internet Explorer also displays BMP files). An image viewer usually displays dozens of graphics formats, many more than a Web browser can han-

dle. Of course, Web browsers can also display HTML files while image viewers are limited to image files.

7. Fixing the broken links.

9. It is generally not possible (or if possible, very expensive) to establish an Internet connection in flight. If you know you want to explore a large Web site during a long flight, you could use a site grabber to download the whole site beforehand, and then view it offline during the flight.

◎◎ Chapter Five

1. JavaScript scripts are inserted inside a `<SCRIPT></SCRIPT>` tag pair inside the `HEAD` element. A `.js` file holds a JavaScript program that can then be referenced by an HTML file. When a script is very long it makes more sense to put it in its own `.js` file.

3. Ideally, one should test for Internet Explorer and Netscape Navigator on both PCs and Macs. If possible, different versions of IE and Navigator should also be tested. Because JavaScript scripts do not always run under both IE and Navigator, professional Web designers often add a test to their Web pages so users running one browser can execute a script written for that browser, while users running a different browser can execute a script written for that one. This is the only way to get around browser incompatibilities without hurting any users.

5. Applets and scripts cannot spread computer viruses; however, they can both pass information back to a Web server. A malicious script is one that does something destructive, such as crashing your system or altering files.

7. Applets are added to Web pages via an `APPLET` or `OBJECT` element. When you download an applet, you download a `.class` file.

9. A data-driven applet is one that displays information stored in a separate text file. Separating out the data for the display makes it easier to update announcements and other information that requires frequent changes.

◎◎ Chapter Six

1. Open source software is software that is distributed along with its source code files. This is distinctly different from most commercial software, which is proprietary: the source code for proprietary software is kept secret.

3. 1992

5. Stallman means software whose source code is distributed freely; it has nothing to do with how much the software costs.

7. Companies that sell open source software are really selling their own documentation or customer support. An example is Red Hat Linux.

9. The award went to the Linux user community. InfoWorld readers cast votes to pick the winner, and this particular award was surprising because it didn't go to a commercial Help Desk operation. Instead, it went to a large user community for its own altruistic support network on message boards and Usenet newsgroups.

INDEX

CREDITS

Figure 1.3	Kookaburra Software (`www.kburra.com`)
Figure 3.9	© 2001 Amazon.com, Inc. All rights reserved.
Figure 3.16	*Waiting for Wendy*
Figures 3.19, 3.20	Used with permission from interMute, Inc. AdSubtract Software available on the Web at `www.adsubtract.com`
Figure 4.3	Arachnophilia is available at `www.arachnoid.com` `<http://www.arachnoid.com>`
Figure 4.8	Cursor Arts Company, `http://www.cursorarts.com`
Figures 4.13, 4.14, 4.15, 4.16, 4.17, 4.18, 4.19	Dr. William T. Verts
Figure 4.25	SiteSucker © 2001 Rick Cranisky (`cranisky@fgm.com`). SiteSucker can be found at `http://members.aol.com/rcranisky/SiteSucker.hqx` or `http://homepage.mac.com/cranisky/SiteSucker.hqx`